EDITORS

Wes Jamison is an associate professor of public relations at Palm Beach Atlantic University, West Palm Beach, Florida, where he teaches, researches persuasive messages in food and agriculture, and directs the Public Relations program. He received a PhD from Oregon State University in agricultural and natural resource politics and has nearly finished his second PhD in public relations from the University of Florida. He is also an ordained Southern Baptist pastor. He has taught for over two decades at universities in Europe and the U.S., travels extensively in the U.S. and internationally giving speeches and papers on his research, and has published extensively in journals, books, and popular publications. He served previously on the governor of Iowa's Biotechnology Task Force and on the board of directors of the Leopold Center of Sustainable Agriculture at Iowa State University.

Paul Copan has a PhD in philosophy from Marquette University, and he is a professor and Pledger Family Chair of Philosophy and Ethics at Palm Beach Atlantic University. He is a philosopher and theologian, and he has authored or edited over thirty-five books, including *"True for You, But Not for Me": Overcoming Objections to Christian Faith*; *An Introduction to Biblical Ethics: Walking in the Way of Wisdom*; *Is God a Moral Monster?: Making Sense of the Old Testament God*; and *The Dictionary of Christianity and Science*. He has contributed to numerous other books and written many journal articles. For six years, he was president of the Evangelical Philosophical Society, and he is also a member of the Institute for Biblical Research.

CONTRIBUTORS

Timothy Hsiao is assistant professor of philosophy at Grantham University and adjunct professor of philosophy at Park University and Johnson County Community College. He works mainly in the area of applied ethics and has published in numerous journals, including the *Journal of Agricultural and Environmental Ethics*, *Public Affairs Quarterly*, and *Ethics & Medicine*. His work has also appeared in a number of popular outlets, including *The Federalist* and *Public Discourse*.

Walter C. Kaiser Jr. has a PhD in Mediterranean studies from Brandeis University. He is president emeritus and Distinguished Professor of Old Testament and Ethics at Gordon-Conwell Theological Seminary in Hamilton, Massachusetts. He is the author of numerous books on the Old Testament, including *Toward Old Testament Ethics* and *What Does the Lord*

Require? He is the son of a farmer; he is now retired and lives with his wife, Nancy, on a farm in Oostburg, Wisconsin.

Gordon Spronk is a native of the Pipestone, Minnesota, agricultural community, and he is a 1981 graduate of the College of Veterinary Medicine, University of Minnesota. Dr. Spronk currently serves as a staff veterinarian and is co-owner of the family farm, with 10,000 sows and over 3,000 corn and soybean acres. His community activities include church elder and trustee of local churches and supporter of several local and regional charities.

Randy Spronk is a pork producer from Edgerton, Minnesota, and is the managing partner for two family farms: Spronk Brothers III LLP (pork production) and Ranger Farms LLP (crop production). The pork production enterprise markets 120,000 head annually, and the crop production consists of corn and soybeans. Spronk served on the NPPC board of directors from 2007 to 2015, serving as president in 2015. Randy served and chaired numerous NPPC committees, including the Trade Policy Committee. Randy continues to represent producers and the industry in a host of venues, such as Congress, the Ag Markets Advisory Council (AMAC), executive council of United States Meat Export Federation (USMEF), and trade shows. He served on the Minnesota Pork Producers Association, serving as president in 1999. He holds a degree in animal science from South Dakota State University.

Thomas J. St. Antoine serves as professor of communication and director of the Frederick M. Supper Honors Program at Palm Beach Atlantic University. Tom has conducted research in the areas of rhetoric and public address, specializing in the rhetoric of place and agrarian rhetoric. He has published his research in a variety of academic books and journals, and he has presented his research at national and regional conferences.

WHAT WOULD JESUS ∧EAT?

Really

The Biblical Case FOR EATING MEAT

EDITORS WES JAMISON, PhD, AND PAUL COPAN, PhD

WHAT WOULD JESUS REALLY EAT? THE BIBLICAL CASE FOR EATING MEAT

All rights reserved
Printed in Canada
978-1-988928-17-3 Soft Cover
978-1-988928-18-0 E-book

Published by: Castle Quay Books
Burlington, Ontario
Riviera Beach, Florida
Tel: (416) 573-3249
E-mail: info@castlequaybooks.com | www.castlequaybooks.com

Edited by Marina Hofman Willard
Cover design and book interior by Burst Impressions
Printed at Essence Printing

Special gratitude is expressed to the AAA (Animal Agriculture Alliance) for making this publication possible by their generous contribution and sponsorship of this book.

Library and Archives Canada Cataloguing in Publication
Title: What would Jesus really eat? : the biblical case for eating meat / editors Wes Jamison, PhD, and Paul Copan, PhD.
Names: Jamison, Wes, 1960- author, editor. | Copan, Paul, author, editor.
Identifiers: Canadiana 20190118814 | ISBN 9781988928173 (softcover)
Subjects: LCSH: Meat—Religious aspects—Christianity. | LCSH: Animal welfare—Religious aspects—Christianity. | LCSH: Vegetarianism—Religious aspects—Christianity. | LCSH: Meat—Biblical
    teaching. | LCSH: Animal welfare—Biblical teaching. | LCSH: Vegetarianism—Biblical teaching.
Classification: LCC BT748 .W43 2019 | DDC 241/.693—dc23

CASTLE QUAY BOOKS

CONTENTS

PREFACE

Each year, late in the autumn after the harvest has been brought in, Americans celebrate the Thanksgiving holiday. Tables around the country are set with a cornucopia of food and treats as citizens join in the annual ritual of giving thanks for the blessings of creation. And even newcomers to the United States recognize the central fixture of the holiday tables—the turkey. Harking back to pre-colonial days, when life was certainly tougher and tenuous, the day reminds people that gratefulness for the Lord's bounty has been an integral part of the United States' moral fabric and collective memory. Ostensibly a Christian holiday first commemorated by the Pilgrims and local native peoples, the images of community and cooperation tug at the heart of the nation's collective identity. But memories fade, moral fabrics sometimes fray, and identities are fluid.

A colleague once had the opportunity to visit the Native American protests at Plymouth Rock, where native peoples and their activist surrogates annually protest the coming of European settlers as the beginning of a continent-wide cultural genocide. They are in effect contesting the accepted meaning of Thanksgiving as a time of peacefulness, blessing, and plenty, instead advocating for an alternative dirge of colonization and exploitation. Nonetheless, when interviewed, they all acknowledged that the focus around which the first celebration centered was food. And to a person, they believed and accepted that consuming animals was central to that celebration. So even activists who abhor the historical cultural narrative of Thanksgiving agree with their traditionalist enemies that animal slaughter and consumption are as old as civilization, whether it be indigenous or immigrant.

This book is about the consumption of meat—and the freedom and joy that Christians can have as they eat it. It is also a primer for non-believers to better understand the ideals that motivate Christians to seemingly overlook animal suffering in their omnivorous diet and instead gleefully eat burgers, barbecue, fried chicken, and an almost endless array of meat supplied by an efficient and overwhelmingly safe production system. This book is also about relatively recent attacks by those who oppose meat-eating and the intensive process that produces the animals that are eaten. Unlike the Native Americans who oppose the Pilgrims but nonetheless rejoice over venison and turkey meat, these activists and philosophers seek to discredit the historical narrative about meat—namely, that meat has been and should remain a central staple of the diet and that the ethical support for eating it is valid.

Attend many dinner celebrations in Western countries, and you find that meat forms an important part of the meal. Known as "center-of-the-plate" or "center-of-the-table," meat in various cultures symbolizes the ability of humans to thrive in their environments, whether they be in the Arctic or the desert, whether in the forests of the Northeastern seaboard or the vast Great Plains of the American West.

But what is meat? In some sense, eating meat literally means eating another animal's muscles and tissues, taking its life to sustain your own. The word itself comes from the Old English word *mete*, which initially meant food in general. With time, the word evolved to mean "food from animals," and then more specifically their flesh. Variations of this meaning are found in various historical studies; Scandinavian languages also held *meat* to mean food in general. However, over time lowland languages like Old Frisian made distinctions between meat as important food versus foods of lesser value, like sweets and vegetables. Thus early European cultures reflected the idea of meat as food, and eventually meat came to mean something more, something central and vital. Hence, at its essence, meat is a nutrient-dense protein pack from animals, which have taken things we *can't* eat and drink—like grass and stagnant water—and converted them into things we *can* eat and drink. In reality, animals link photosynthesis to human stomachs: animals eat plants (and sometimes other animals and insects) and convert them to edible and tasty products for human enjoyment. They scavenge and forage, root and winnow, as they seek out and find nutrients to feed themselves, and which ultimately feed us. For many thousands of years, people have used animals in much the same way.

And yet, a chorus of voices claims that meat-eating is ethically questionable at best and morally repugnant at worst. As readers will discover, a few decades ago animal protectionists identified religion as a target exactly because religion forms the core of a person's beliefs. If beliefs lead to attitudes that lead to behaviors, then any activist who wants to end animal production, slaughter, and consumption must attack beliefs at their religious core. In this, Christianity is somewhat unique because both its religious tradition and the Bible itself provide permission to raise and eat animals and to do so freely, with joy—not unlike the Pilgrims who celebrated God's gracious provision with a feast. It's no mistake that we eat turkey at Thanksgiving.

But the opponents of such a view have made concerted efforts to undermine and overturn this freedom. They claim that the Bible does not teach what we think it teaches about animal production and consumption, and they claim that religious tradition is resplendent with examples of believers who abandoned meat-eating in favor of a more compassionate, less cruel lifestyle. And they do this in sophisticated and nuanced ways that can leave Christian meat-eaters at a loss for words—much less arguments—to defend what they have taken for granted: namely, that meat-eating is not only good but right, that their consumption choices are not matters of conscience but rather matters of freedom and enjoyment and gratitude.

Hence, ultimately this book is a resource for those Christians who seek a defense of their freedom to raise, slaughter, and consume animals while worshiping God and giving thanks for his bountiful provision. They are faced with words that sound like Sunday school lessons from long ago, confronted with Scripture verses that are removed from their context but nonetheless sound appealing, and vexed by opponents who claim to be just like them—believers in the Lord Jesus Christ. And yet these new voices proclaim a better and more enlightened way. No wonder Christians can become frustrated. After all, they *know* what they believe, but perhaps they just don't know *why* they believe it or *how* to defend their beliefs. This book is for them.

———

The book is divided into five sections, each written and intended to provide insight and understanding into the debate surrounding Christianity and animal production and consumption. Part I discusses why words matter—or how the rhetoric and arguments themselves guide and frame the debate. If the words we choose to discuss issues of importance to us really do matter, then understanding the language used in the debate becomes very important. Part II discusses how animal rights activists, philosophers, and apologists have intentionally targeted Christian beliefs and attempted to redefine key concepts in Christianity toward a more sympathetic perspective for their cause. In effect, this issue matters to Christians exactly because it not only denies thousands of years of human experience but could potentially undermine religious support for their diet.

Part III discusses at length why eating meat is morally appropriate—but the focus is on why people matter. So much of the rhetoric and activism of opponents proposes a leveling and blurring of the differences between people and animals, and a chief pillar for Christian belief is human uniqueness and specialness in creation. And part IV reveals why Scripture matters, providing involved analysis of what the Bible actually says about God, people, and animals and the relationship between the three. Two theologians present what is of critical importance to the Christian—namely, a useful overview of the biblical permission and mandate to use animals—and thus provide comfort for the believer who just wants to enjoy what God has given. Finally, part V answers the question "Can a Christian farm, slaughter, and eat animals and still rejoice in God's will?" through the perspective of a Christian farming family that raises pigs.

Can Christians be animal farmers, even on a large highly efficient farm? Can they work in a processing plant, or a grocery store, or a BBQ restaurant, or even as a homemaker who feeds the family with nutritious and healthy meat? Can they do so with clear consciences, with joy and thanksgiving, even in the face of attacks on their beliefs by opponents? Can a believer rest in the knowledge that God, as revealed in the Bible, is not only permissive but pleased when they settle in for a plate of meat? This book seeks to answer those questions and, in the words of the old Dutch hymn, provide guidance and comfort:

> We gather together to ask the Lord's blessing;
> He chastens and hastens His will to make known;
> The wicked oppressing now cease from distressing;
> Sing praises to His Name; He forgets not His own.

PART I
Why Words Matter

1. You Are What You Say You Eat
THOMAS J. ST. ANTOINE

In the beginning was the Word,
and the Word was with God,
and the Word was God.
(John 1:1)

People love to talk about food. They always have. We all know someone—
or perhaps we are someone—who loves to discuss all aspects of food.
There are entire television networks dedicated to food shows. We have
our celebrity chefs who model "food talk" for us. We buy cookbooks,
books about the latest diets, and books about the political and economic
consequences of our food choices. In New Orleans, which is perhaps the
American city most self-conscious and passionate about its food culture,
there is a radio talk show dedicated to all things food. While other
American radio hosts are taking calls about politics, sports, and popular
culture, listeners in New Orleans are calling in to discuss the newest
restaurant in the French Quarter, who makes the best oysters Rockefeller,
or how to prepare that redfish caught in the Gulf last weekend.

We have conversations about what we have eaten in the past and what
we plan to eat in the future. We talk about what we like, what we don't
like, and what we would like to try. We tell stories about our favorite places
to eat. We talk about how food is prepared. We discuss the ingredients in
food and whether those ingredients are good for our health or bad for
our health. Finally, we express our identity through food, whether we are
gluten-averse hipsters or butter-loving biscuits-and-gravy Southerners.
Some people choose not to eat meat in order to communicate their
sympathies with animals or with the environment or to express concern
about the scarcity of resources. Others wonder whether it is necessary or
even possible to express their faith through the choices they make in the
grocery store, the restaurant, or the kitchen.

These first two chapters examine the power of food talk. The Greeks created the word *rhetoric* to refer to the art of persuasion. Today, the rhetoric of food has shaped our perceptions about what we eat and where it comes from. In the last 20 years, a number of bestsellers, movies, and publicity campaigns have both subtly and not so subtly changed the way we eat. As Christians ask the question "What would Jesus eat?" it is important to remember that this is an ongoing conversation with established arguments for the ethics and politics of eating. In these chapters, I intend to bring to light those arguments and demonstrate the power of rhetoric to determine where this conversation will go next.

While this book explores the place of animals in God's creation and the role that we as humans are called to play in their stewardship, this chapter and the next serve as a backdrop to these discussions. They introduce the reader to the nature of rhetoric and the role it has played in establishing our taken-for-granted assumptions about animals and food.

THE POWER AND POTENTIAL OF RHETORIC

Talk is not cheap. Our use of language allows us to be like God. As People of the Book, Christians understand the significance of "the Word." God spoke his creation into existence, and having created us in his image, God has passed on to us his capacity to create as well. Like God, we use language to create. The act of naming something is an act of creation. When we choose to name something "good" or "heroic" or "honorable," we assign meaning and value to it. We prescribe the proper actions that one is to take relative to that construct. Our words bring us together to create communities, and they also divide us, creating sub-communities. Words make some people powerful and others powerless. Labels create understanding, and they can create *mis*understanding. Our culture, values, and actions rely on our naming of things and ideas, and it is critical that we approach this power with seriousness and reverence. Recognizing that our ideas and the words we use to identify them have consequences, Richard Weaver wrote, "a soul which is rightly affected calls that good which is good; but a soul which is wrongly turned calls that good which is evil."[1]

In today's advertising, political rhetoric, public relations, digital media, interpersonal communication, and so many other places, we can see rhetoric in action. Whether or not we are conscious of it, we are constantly exposed to rhetorical arguments. They shape our understanding of the world, and they serve as motives for action. There is no shortage of news reports, blogs, books, and conversations pointing out the state of our over-communicated society. Persuasive messages are inescapable. Every time we pick up our electronic devices, we are targeted with ads and enticements to click or to buy or to post or to vote. Even if we try to unplug and go for a walk, we are likely to pass a bus with an advertisement or a park bench with some persuasive message. Rhetoric is inescapable.

The tools of the persuader are varied, and we see these strategies on full display in the rhetoric of food. Once a persuader—perhaps an animal welfare activist, a spokesperson for the food industry, an advertiser, a scholar, or a PR consultant—gains access to the consumer, the persuasion begins. Our discussions of food are filled with many kinds of persuasive appeals. Whether you have noticed or not, you have been presented with arguments about what food you should eat, where it should come from, and what the consequences of your food choices are.

THE RHETORIC OF FOOD

In the last decade, a variety of books has been published on the politics, ethics, and health values of food. These books have covered everything from the production to the processing to the consumption of food. We have long known that we express the values of a culture through food. International foods like Italian, Mediterranean, or Mexican and regional foods like Southern, Cajun, or Tex-Mex all tell us about the climate of their region of origin. The ingredients reflect the plants and animals that thrive there. The preparation tells us about the attentiveness, prosperity, creativity, or hospitality of the region. And the circumstances in which the food is consumed tell us about the region's love for family and parties and guests, its appreciation for luxury, and its outlook on life. Further, all of these things tell us about the identity of those people who produce, prepare, and consume it.

In recent years, however, a number of authors have highlighted the political consequences of our food choices. Recent trends like farm-to-table foods, local/regional agriculture, sustainability, veganism, and others have captured the attention of eater-activists. Several popular books and films have influenced this conversation and have introduced a vocabulary that animates today's arguments about what we ought to be eating.

In 2001, journalist Eric Schlosser captured the public's attention with the publication of *Fast Food Nation*. Schlosser's work calls attention to a wide variety of objections to the fast food industry, including economic injustices, environmental concerns, and problems with the corporatization and industrialization of food.[2] This movement gained momentum in 2004, when Morgan Spurlock's film *Super Size Me* made a splash by condemning fast food, mostly on the grounds of health, but it also attempted to induce guilt for a gluttonous American lifestyle. In that film, Spurlock can be seen debating with his vegan girlfriend and defending moderate consumption of meat.[3] Michael Pollan, a journalist and advocate for local foods, first published *The Omnivore's Dilemma* in 2006. Since then, he has published a variety of other books on the industrial food system, including *In Defense of Food*. Pollan's work attempts to connect our food choices with an array of consequences, including cultural, moral, political, environmental, and economic conditions.[4]

In 2008, Robert Kenner produced *Food, Inc.,* a documentary film on large corporate agribusiness. This film and its companion book lay out an argument for the deleterious economic and health effects of the food industry; they claim that all segments of American society—poor, middle class, consumers, farmers, and others—suffer negative consequences at the hands of powerful corporations involved in agribusiness, food processing, and marketing.[5] That same year, Paul Roberts—another journalist—published *The End of Food*, in which he identifies the dangers and shortcomings of the mass production of food, forecasting that the system is not sustainable and will either collapse or become prohibitively costly.[6]

The following year, Hank Cardello, a former executive in the food industry who worked at food companies including Coca Cola and General Mills, published a book called *Stuffed*. It reveals the tactics and resources used by the food industry to convince the public to buy their products. Cardello describes Americans' unlimited quest to buy more than they need and to consume foods that are not good for them.[7] In 2013, Jayson Lusk, an agriculture economics professor, wrote *The Food Police: A Well-Fed Manifesto About the Politics of Your Plate*. He points out the idealism and hypocrisy of authors who have led the charge to modify the way we produce, distribute, and eat our food. This book makes an argument in support of modern agribusiness against the wave of critics cited in this section.[8]

This small sample gives a sense of the range of best-selling books and films critiquing our contemporary food system. One may speculate on the cause of this interest, but it remains clear that this topic has been central to modern popular discourse.

Industry and interest groups have responded in calculated ways to the public conversation about food production and consumption. High-profile groups like the Humane Society of the United States (HSUS) have been active in addressing these issues. One effort in particular—Faith Outreach—has sought to engage religious audiences in the animal welfare movement in a general way by aligning the HSUS with orthodox religious beliefs. The Faith Outreach initiative has a website with videos featuring respected evangelical Christians. It also includes ads for films on religion and animals as well as information on the "faith councils" made up of experts from a variety of religious people and groups who have committed to defending animal welfare issues.[9]

The HSUS "Facts and Faith" page features a library of religious statements on animals that includes formal positions from the major religions—Christianity, Judaism, Hinduism, Buddhism, and Islam. The Christian statements include documents from twelve major denominations. Those statements are fairly uniform and include a short paragraph on the history and identity of that particular faith tradition, the denomination's official statements on animals (including that tradition's animal-related prayers and services), and remarks from that denomination's leaders.[10] Finally, the HSUS superintended an effort to make an Evangelical statement on animals, to circulate it, and to have evangelicals sign it in support. That effort resulted in creating a website of its own, Every Living Thing, which includes the statement and an explanatory essay along with additional information.[11]

RHETORICAL POSSIBILITIES

A rhetorical theory known as the "narrative paradigm" is a widely accepted critical lens for understanding rhetoric, and it applies to our discussion of food. Walter Fisher suggests that narrative can explain how rhetoric and persuasion appeal to their audiences.[12] And it is no surprise that, in the struggle to define our terms, narrative is a key construct in arguments about the production and consumption of food. To call something "fresh from the farm" or "homemade" tells us something about the quality of the food, but it also implies a story about where your food came from, who produced it, and how it was produced. The food we eat always tells a story. Every item on your plate implies an *origin*. The consumer is given some explanation as to how it was produced and where it came from. Often the story includes indications of how the animals that produced this food lived and how they died. It implies a method of harvest and distribution. The consumer may envision a pleasant pastoral scene that includes animals being raised on a traditional farm—or she might assume a more industrial method of production.

The food we eat also implies something about *preparation*. We might be told how it was harvested and processed—or that it was served fresh, after loving and expert preparation by a chef. The eater might also learn whether the food was prepared with substances to preserve it or to enhance its taste and texture. The story might indicate whether the food was stored for a long time and how it was preserved and distributed. Some items come from far away in a shipping container while others, the story goes, are produced nearby and arrive in the back of a farmer's truck.

All of these details are elements that form a rich, coherent story for the public. This is the story of food, the story of animals, the story of farmers and laborers, the story of restaurant owners, and the story of eaters.

One might ask why these stories matter. They matter because these small stories connect to and resonate with larger metanarratives or "grand stories" such as the story of God, of his creation, and of his relationship with humankind. These stories help us make sense of our rights and responsibilities as consumers. They provide a framework for discussing the morality and ethics of food production and consumption. They help us to understand the nature of things like animals and agriculture. These stories provide a vocabulary we can use to engage in the pervasive cultural discourse about what we "ought" to be eating. Finally, these stories pull back the curtain on the arguments, many of which may have gone undetected, that have led us to accept a variety of assumptions about food.

In the pages that follow, you will read arguments about how we, as Christians, allegedly ought to eat. In the process, we may find that we— or perhaps well-meaning Christians we know—have adopted a false or misguided compassion rather than genuine biblical compassion. Without knowing it, perhaps we—or they—have been trying to be more "spiritual" than Jesus himself.

We will consider which narrative is most aligned with God's plan for the world—that is, the one that best enables us to love and serve our neighbors and thus honor his creation. Then we will think about the ways in which we can most faithfully live out the authoritative biblical narrative both as producers and as consumers. To do so, we will be asked to consider the appropriateness of placing ourselves into these narratives about a food's origin, preparation, and consumption. The arguments we examine acknowledge that our food has a story. Some of those stories will resonate with the believer as exhibiting Christian virtue. Others will imply vice.[13]

2. Basic Ingredients
THOMAS J. ST. ANTOINE

The narratives that have shaped our current understanding of food produced a vocabulary that introduces the public to some new words, changes the meaning of others, and divides the public based on how they value and define contested terms. To be sure, these words have creative power. They give shape to how we act and how we eat. These terms have become buzzwords, jargon, and labels used to create an understanding of the production and consumption of food. The same words that are positive terms for some represent pure evil for others. They are often ambiguous, allowing interest groups to define and then redefine them in ways that best suit their agendas. Opposing sides compete for the right to define them and to advance their view of these terms in the public. These words produce what might be called "manufactured consent," a commonly held, taken-for-granted understanding shared by audiences. We know that the groups that win the contest to define these terms in public acquire a great deal of power and legitimacy in the rhetorical food fight.

The "contested terms" in this chapter reflect a range of views, and they are the basic ingredients used to express the narratives noted in chapter 1. As this book's title suggests, before we can determine "what Jesus would *really* eat," we ought to become more familiar with the basic vocabulary used to discuss the decisive issues. These are the terms that have been created and popularized by industry leaders, journalists, activists, and religious leaders, and they have shaped our culture's attitudes toward food.

AGRARIAN

If you have ever read a story or seen a movie or had a conversation that implies that "life on the farm" was simpler, more honest, and otherwise better than urban life, you have experienced agrarian language. Deeply rooted in American culture is this set of claims about the goodness of life in the country, on the frontier, and on the farm. The American agrarian philosophical tradition has its roots in the assumption that the modern obsession with efficiency, quantity, technique, and economies of scale have not served us well. It is also a rebellion against technological materialism and industrial consumerism. This suspicion is fed by the tendency to promote the traditional farm and agri-"culture" as the height of American virtue. Literary figures such as Wendell Berry, Robert Penn Warren, and Richard Weaver represent the literary and philosophical traditions of agrarianism in America. Perhaps feeding the appeal of their writings is the fact that agrarian images and metaphors are used throughout the Scriptures.[1]

Agrarian arguments have entered into public discourse about food in a number of ways. Michael Pollan uses the term *supermarket pastoral* to refer to the literary genre that conjures a rich narrative in which the American family farmer is the hero who stands against agribusiness. He describes this as a seductive literary form that is often used by "grocery store poets" to create demand for foods produced on traditional farms. He adds, "taken as a whole, the story on offer in Whole Foods is a pastoral narrative in which farm animals live much as they did in the books we read as children, and our fruits and vegetables grow in well-composted soils on small farms."[2]

Appeals to our agrarian heritage can be found in a 2013 video produced by HSUS entitled *A Pig's Tail*. The video makes the argument that animal consumption is morally acceptable in the context of traditional animal husbandry, in which the farmer raises animals humanely and in a pastoral setting. In the most direct reference to agrarianism in the HSUS video, the young pig's mother tells him, "That is a place called the 'old farm' where the sun shines and there are fields of grass with muddy puddles and barns of fresh straw."[3] The old farm is described as a place "where a pig can be a pig and a farmer can be a proud and happy farmer." Put simply, agrarian vocabularies contend that the animals we eat ought to come from traditional farms where the family says grace before a meal, lives simply, and relies on God and neighbor.

AGRIBUSINESS

The industrialization of food production is referred to as "agribusiness." Environmental advocates and food activists have criticized the large-scale technological corporate production of food as unwholesome in a number of ways. Now, agribusiness has offered robust replies in self-defense, but what are some of these criticisms?

For some, agribusiness is emblematic of corporate materialism and greed, which place profits over transcendent goods. One mainline Presbyterian denomination—the PC (U.S.A.)—published a document, advanced by the HSUS, that states, "the integrity of life, including animal life, is more important than economic growth and material consumption."[4] Agribusiness has responded by redefining itself through extensive public relations and advertising efforts. Author Hank Cardello observes, "Because there's so much at stake, food industry groups use their resources to appear everywhere there are decisions to be made about what we eat."[5]

Opponents demonstrate a basic distrust for agribusiness, lamenting that people are no longer connected to the processes that provide their food. The modern industrial food system with its processing plants and concentration of waste became so ugly and smelly and noisy that people didn't want to see it in their backyards. The result was to confine it in specialized zones, away from residential areas. Food was produced on large-scale industrial farms and marketed in pleasant suburban grocery stores. Once American agribusiness was pushed out of the view of the public, however, its remoteness led to mistrust.[6]

Denunciation of the term *agribusiness* can be a rejection of industrialization itself, especially as it has encroached on our agrarian traditions. This extended example is the opening monologue of the film *Food, Inc.* On display here you will see all of the themes in the popular anti-industrial rhetoric of food including a critique of industrialization, accompanied by its greed, deception, artificiality, and exploitation:

The way we eat has changed more in the past 50 years than in the previous 10,000. But the image that's used to sell the food is still the image of agrarian America. You even go into the supermarket and you see pictures of farmers, the picket fence, the silo, the '30s farmhouse and the green grass. It's the spinning of this pastoral fantasy. The modern American supermarket has on average 47,000 products. There are no seasons in the American supermarket. Now there are tomatoes all year round, grown halfway around the world, picked when it was green and ripened with ethylene gas. Although it looks like a tomato, it's kind of a notional tomato. I mean, it's the idea of a tomato. In the meat aisle, there are no bones anymore. There is this deliberate veil, this curtain, that's dropped between us and where our food is coming from. The industry doesn't want you to know the truth about what you are eating, because if you knew, you might not want to eat it. If you follow the food chain back from those shrink-wrapped packages of meat you find a very different reality. The reality is a factory. It's not a farm. It's a factory. That meat is being processed by huge multinational corporations that have very little to do with ranches and farmers. Now our food is coming from enormous assembly lines where the animals and the workers are being abused. And the food has become much more dangerous in ways that are being deliberately hidden from us. You've got a small group of multinational corporations who control the entire food system.[7]

This framing of industrial food and its marketing can be seen in other authors as well. Wendell Berry writes, only half-jokingly, "The food industrialists have by now persuaded millions of consumers to prefer food that is already prepared. They will grow, deliver, and cook your food for you and (just like your mother) beg you to eat it."[8] He later adds that in food advertising the "food wears as much makeup as the actors."[9]

ORGANIC/SUSTAINABLE

Juxtaposed to industrial foods produced by agribusiness, organic and sustainable foods have become very popular in grocery stores, in restaurants, and in green markets that have sprouted up in downtowns everywhere. The terms *organic* and *sustainable* both denote foods grown in cooperation with nature rather than in pursuing mastery over nature. What they connote is the opposite of "artificial" foods. Advocates express concern that modern farming techniques lead to less-healthy soil, less-healthy eaters, and less-healthy economies. Supporters of organic and small-scale agriculture worry that chemicals and pesticides and other technologies have become so necessary that farmers cannot succeed without them. Advertisers have also seized on the popularity of these terms to make their products more desirable. These terms are often used in advertising as nebulous, ambiguous appeals to consumers. Some food activists even fear the popularity of the green movement or the organic label because it allows modern industrial agriculture to market their products under these labels and persist without fundamental change.[10]

Although similar, these two methods of production are distinct. Organic foods are produced and distributed without the use of industrial products and technologies, especially chemicals such as fertilizers and pesticides and genetically modified products like seeds. Sustainability, on the other hand, is offered as a solution to the possible collapse of our overly complex, interdependent food system, and it is pursued by the small, local farming movement. It is possible to be a small-scale local farmer (sustainable) who grows multiple crops but sparingly uses fertilizer or seed that is not organic. Likewise, it is possible to be a large-scale (not sustainable) mono-crop grower who uses large-scale organic methods known as "industrial organic."[11]

VEGAN

The term *vegan* has become part of our contemporary vernacular speech. It denotes a wide variety of positions taken by consumers toward animals based on a variety of convictions. Vegans exercise a number of options including using no animal products whatsoever. This includes an all-vegetable-based diet, but vegans also choose not to consume other animal products, including leather and clothing made from animals. They also avoid products that are tested on animals or that otherwise exploit animals in their manufacture. Vegetarians may use animal products but eat an all-vegetable diet, and some consumers will make exceptions to their diets like eggs or fish.

Vegans make this commitment for a variety of reasons. Many make this decision out of a concern for animal welfare. Others avoid meat for health reasons. Still others avoid meat and animal products out of a concern for scarce resources, based on the assumption that animal products introduce inefficiency into the system, using more feed, land, and fuel to support animal agriculture. This conservation of energy is why "vegetarians advocate eating 'low on the food chain.'"[12] Many vegans base their conviction on some combination of these concerns, criticizing animal agriculture for unjustly allowing the use of animal products to deplete resources, to exploit consumers, to undermine public health, and to mistreat animals.

ANIMAL WELFARE

Discussions of animal welfare have led to an increased sensitivity to the right relationship between humans and animals. Just as authors throughout history have contemplated the idea of the good life for humankind, we in the modern age also wonder whether animals can have a good life and what role humans should play in alleviating the suffering of animals. Wendell Berry remarks, "Though I am by no means a vegetarian, I dislike the thought that some animal has been made miserable in order to feed me. If I am going to eat meat, I want it to be from an animal that has lived a pleasant, uncrowded life outdoors, on bountiful pasture, with good water nearby and trees for shade ... Some, I know, will think it bloodthirsty or worse to eat a fellow creature you have known all its life. On the contrary, I think it means that you eat with understanding and with gratitude."[13]

The HSUS has collaborated with faith communities in their Faith Outreach initiative. The mission of the Faith Outreach, as described by the HSUS, is to "engage people and institutions of faith with animal-protection issues on the premise that religious values call upon us to act in a kind and merciful way towards all creatures."[14] Christians who have participated in the Faith Initiative conceive of the relationship between humans and animals as a reflection of God's relationship with us. Just as God loves his creation, we love our pets. If believers are called to love others, they can learn to do so by loving animals. Likewise, it is suggested that we can express our love for God by loving his creation. As the argument goes, we can become more loving human beings and can learn to love others by loving animals. Conversely, we can diminish ourselves when we "mistreat" animals.

Christians are called to love the least of these, and the HSUS positions animals as such. Animals are called "especially vulnerable" and "most subject to irresponsible and cruel treatment by humans." The Evangelical statement (see chapter 1) claims that humans abuse animals because humanity is fallen and all human relationships are corrupted: "We believe that when sin entered the world through human rebellion it corrupted all relationships, firstly between humanity and God, but also relationships between people and between humankind and animals."[15] The statement goes on to say, "as we live in a fallen world and are prone to sin, we also have the capacity and inclination to cause suffering instead of care for animals and to act cruelly towards them."[16] Conversely, when we love animals we "reflect His rule and character."[17] Although humankind is fallen, it is also created in God's image and can love his creation as he loves us. The Episcopal statement puts it more colorfully: Anyone who "will not be merciful to his beast, is a beast himself."[18] The HSUS illustrates this idea with statements from credible voices in contemporary Christian culture. Eric Metaxas, for example, cites William Wilberforce, who argued that mistreating animals coarsens humankind, and credits Wilberforce and his Christian convictions with the genesis of the animal activist movement.[19]

STEWARDSHIP/DOMINION

We are concerned about animal welfare because animals are created by God, please him, and are part of God's "very good" world. Humans are distinct from animals but share in the responsibility for their care. *Dominion* is a contested term that distinguishes responsible care from exploitation. The Catholic and Baptist statements both separate humanity from animals, calling humanity the pinnacle of creation, which receives animals as a gift for responsible use. A finer distinction is also made in identifying the created order as still in the possession of God, and, even as humans are stewards, they are caretakers of *God's*—not *their*—possession. The traditional arguments about dominion are refined in the Evangelical statement, which uses the term *radah* to describe a dominion that "respects the one being ruled." The statement elaborates, "God is the ultimate owner of not only the earth, but all its inhabitants … [H]umans have rule over the animals; they ultimately belong, like all of creation, to God. Thus by implication, we are responsible to Him for how we treat them."[20] The Methodist statement illustrates the effort to reframe and reform the term *dominion*: "we have confused God's call for us to be faithful stewards of creation with a license to use all of creation as we see fit" and must "repent of our devastation of the physical nonhuman world," keeping in mind that God's "covenant is with all creatures."[21]

I have worked with focus groups made up of active believers who discussed animal welfare issues. In these focus groups and elsewhere, Christian responses have expressed fundamental concerns about animal dominion and the order it implies. They express that while a basic kindness to animals is good, it is not the greatest good. It is a worldly, temporal good that is outweighed by the eternal. The love of God and neighbor outweighs a love of creation. The archbishop of Mosul, for example, drew attention when he criticized Christians in the West for paying more attention to animal rights than to the plight of persecuted and martyred Christians throughout the world.[22] This mirrors the response of many conservative Christians who worry that our culture of death laments the mistreatment of animals while we neglect human suffering caused by injustice, sin, and disorder.

NATURE/CREATION

Natural is used as both an advertising and a philosophical term. A consequence of the fall resulted in a drastic change in the relationship between humans and nature. Before the fall, Adam and Eve lived in the garden-park of Eden to work and enjoy all that God provided for them there. Work—a gift from God—was still necessary because certain natural forces needed to be kept back or "subdued" (*kabash*). Just think of the simple weeding and pruning to be done in our own gardens.

As our book shows elsewhere, our first parents were protected from natural perils—predatory animals, earthquakes, tornadoes—while they maintained fellowship with God. But because of the fall, they—and now we—have become vulnerable to these natural forces that were already in place before the fall. In addition, our *work* has now become *toil*, and we must labor and strive to make the land productive. And humanity has done harm to the natural world through pollution and the abuse of natural resources.

Some Christians have the impression that the original created order did not mean work and that no pushing back of certain natural processes was necessary. This view is much like the ancient classical tradition. The Roman writer Ovid described a golden age:

> Earth willingly, untouched, unwounded yet
> By hoe or plough, gave all her bounteous store;
> Men were content with nature's food unforced.

In a later, corrupted period, that harmony was lost:

> And on the ground, common till then and free
> As air and sunlight, far across the fields
> By careful survey boundaries were marked.
> Nor did earth's rich return of crops and food
> Suffice...[23]

What is clear is that our harmonious existence with nature is no longer a reality. Yet, we seem to desire an eternal return to that which is "natural." Many diets provide the guidance that if it is found in nature, we should eat it. If it was produced in a lab, we should avoid it. Conversely, it is true that many poisons and toxins are found in nature, while vitamins can be produced in laboratories. Christians have expressed an uneasy relationship with the natural world, recognizing nature as God's creation while being mindful of its temporality and subjection to decay and death. Romans 8:19–21 describes creation as being "subjected to futility" and in "slavery to corruption" and undergoing "the anxious longing" to be redeemed. Genesis 3:17–19 depicts this transformation from *work* to *toil* and from *harmony* in Eden to *vulnerability* to natural forces:

> "Cursed is the ground because of you;
> In toil you will eat of it
> All the days of your life.
> Both thorns and thistles it shall grow for you;
> And you will eat the plants of the field;
> By the sweat of your face
> You will eat bread,
> Till you return to the ground,
> Because from it you were taken;
> For you are dust,
> And to dust you shall return."

The Evangelical statement circulated by the HSUS acknowledges that animals and humans are both part of the created order, and animals reveal the nature of the Creator to us: "We believe that all animals ultimately belong to God, are sustained by Him, and exist to bring Him praise and reveal His character."[24] The Catholic statement elaborates, "Animals should be respected because each contains the 'imprint of the Creator' and reflects 'a ray of God's infinite wisdom and goodness.'"[25] Human interaction with animals, then, reveals the human condition and illuminates man's relationship with his Creator.

At the same time, great effort is made to distinguish animals from humans. According to the Evangelical statement, "We believe God uniquely created humankind in His own image and likeness, in contrast to creatures ... who are created after their own kind."[26] One of the consistent objections of Christians is that the animal welfare movement, rooted in evolutionary biology and even paganism, does not recognize the great chain of being in which humankind, possessing God's image—with its moral, spiritual, volitional, linguistic, and cultural capacities—is set apart from the animals. The HSUS counters with the claim that one can support animal welfare without being vegan and that we need not worship animals or place them on equal ground with humans to love them. The explanatory essay that accompanies the Evangelical statement rejects "any attempt to idolize or divinize animals and be vigilant against this distortion."[27] For others, the pleasure of eating, the consumption of creation, is sacramental. Berry concludes his essay,

> Eating with the fullest pleasure—pleasure, that is, that does not depend on ignorance—is perhaps the profoundest enactment of our connection with the world. In this pleasure we experience and celebrate our dependence and our gratitude, for we are living from mystery, from creatures we did not make and powers we cannot comprehend.[28]

EPILOGUE: WORDS MATTER, INDEED

In popular discourse, the definitions of key terms are often open and uncertain. We have an emotional attachment or opposition to these contested terms even if we don't know what they mean. Until we carefully define these terms, they remain empty emotional triggers. Who, after all, isn't opposed to cruelty to animals? No one would oppose good stewardship or nature or animal welfare. The problem is that we have not taken the time to debate what constitutes cruelty and why it's cruel, what nature is, and how Christians should interact with it. If we become more aware of these terms and vocabularies, we are better equipped to take up the issues we will find in this book and to discuss the complex, multifaceted, and sometimes contradictory question "What would Jesus *really* eat?"

PART II
WHY THE ISSUE MATTERS

3. Pigs, Peas, and Seals:
The Universality of Meat-Eating
WES JAMISON

THREE VIGNETTES

Barbeque is a little bit like love. When it's done just right, the sensations bring a pleasure that is unique in all the world. Attending a cook-off, you hear the affection the chefs and customers have for their meat, describing the meal in rapturous tones. The look in their eyes reveals sweet contentment as they moan with approval. At a renowned BBQ contest, after eating a particularly pleasurable rack of ribs, one local noted, "There's a reason they call it comfort food." And although any ensuing guilt probably involves the level of calories consumed rather than the animals consumed, rarely if ever are heard the lamentations of the faithful that somehow their meals were in violation of the local Baptist church's sermon that day.

Katie is a waitress at Dianne's Old Time Barbeque, a restaurant in north Florida that joins in the fun of BBQ competitions. She is the granddaughter of the founder of one of the South's most famous BBQ chains, so she knows something about eating animals. When asked why her meat is so delicious, what makes her dishes unique, why so many customers on their way somewhere else make it a point to stop and dine with her, Katie answers simply, "It's the meat ..."—and smiling, she adds, "and the cook!" Katie herself fits the image: the twang of the rural South mingled with the bonhomie of a laid-back rural lifestyle, without any ethical misgivings about her work. Sure, she's got problems, but cooking, serving, or eating massive amounts of animals isn't one of them.

Far away, suburban Washington exudes sophistication and power. Laden with restaurants, DC speaks of its utility as a place for power lunches and networking, as those with power plan their agenda. In one such place sits Christine, a highly educated and motivated urban professional who is passionate about herself and the cause of animal rights. A vegetarian, she makes a point of telling everyone that hers is a religious choice. And even though health plays an important part, she believes that eating right and eating good are the same thing. More important, her religion guides her interactions with a world rife with industrial animal agriculture. She is clear that she believes animals are treated poorly on factory farms and that their treatment is morally wrong. She is politically active—an "elite" in the world of animal protection who has blended her religious beliefs into her life in a seamless constellation that provides comfort and meaning. Nothing if not moralistic, she expresses her compassion publicly by not eating animals. She says, "If Christians knew how their compassionate God protects animals, they would think again about their eating decisions!"

Interestingly, both Katie and Christine claim to be Christians who derive their beliefs about eating animals from heartfelt religious principles; their beliefs are rooted in a mixture of church teaching, biblical principles, and tradition that many Americans claim as their moral compass. But one eats pigs while the other eats peas. And although Katie's beliefs might seem to be more culturally religious, located in the buckle of the Bible Belt, Christine reflects the growing chorus of voices that challenge whether eating animals, especially animals from intensive confinement, is the right thing to do. And she expressly feels called to spread the bad news— the anti-gospel that Christian compassion for the suffering of animals overrules any freedoms believers think they have to exploit animals— coupled with the good news that vegetarianism is a godlier choice.

In an annual Thanksgiving holiday rite symbolizing not only America's bounty but the success of agricultural industrialization, the National Turkey Federation presents the first family with a living turkey. In due course, the president makes some obligatory comments commemorating that first pre-colonial meat-centered celebration, then pardons the fowl, sparing at least one lucky turkey's neck from the chopping block. Encapsulated in one perfect, ironic moment, modern society's discomfort over eating dead animals confronts consumers on the national stage. I was once engaged in a rather humorous conversation at a local DC watering hole with a spokesperson for the turkey industry, and a unique idea surfaced regarding a campaign to deny clemency to the "national turkey." The idea was to reconnect the turkey in the photo op to the meat in the butcher shop. Scoffing, the lobbyist dismissed the idea: "Just because people eat turkey doesn't mean they want to meet the bird!"

In many ways, 21st-century America is schizophrenic about its meat. On the one hand, we eat 250 million turkeys per year, most of them consumed in our collective celebrations and rituals, while, on the other hand, we blanch at the thought of their demise. The numbers of animals raised annually in the U.S. for meat are staggering: over 120 million pigs, 150 million cattle, 8 billion chickens, an estimated 9.5 billion animals altogether. And yet the reality of the process of converting those animals into pork, steak, and fryers has been largely hidden from the culture's collective consciousness. Indeed, a speaker at an animal rights conference said that the only factor that allowed animal agriculture to survive was the ability of meat-eaters to live out the adage "out of sight, out of mind." Similarly, a visit to the Animal Liberation Front website affords a front-row seat to the discourse attacking the schizophrenia: "If slaughterhouses had glass walls, we would all be vegetarian." Implicit in those criticisms is the belief that meat-eating is wrong, abhorrent, and morally repugnant, that it is somehow an aberration from the normal and normative state of nature.

Is meat-eating ethical? An anthropologist colleague recounted his trip to the Arctic and a seal meat dinner shared by firelight. When asked whether they thought that consuming seals was wrong, the Inuit answered that eating animals was what they did; it was natural and normal. They were no exception. On the other side of the planet, the locals have dogs as pets *and* eat them too! Titcomb's *Dog and Man in the Ancient Pacific* tells how Pacific Islanders viewed Europeans, who lived with companion animals and *did not* eat them, as simply wasteful and weird![1]

MEAT-EATING AND ETHICS

These anecdotes illustrate both the normal, natural biological activity of meat-eating and the cultural relativity of food ethics. It is beyond dispute that humans developed as omnivores. Throughout history, people have shown remarkable environmental adaptability that has allowed them to live in inhospitable habitats and marginal lands where animals are either the only source of food or the only mechanism that can convert inedible plants and undrinkable water into food. Simply put, animals take nature that people can't use and convert it into things people must use. So just declaring a natural human biological activity unethical based on political or personal opinion is a legalism more in keeping with religious hypocrites, secular Pharisees, and cultural imperialists than with Christian beliefs.

One presumed purpose of ethics is to constrain and channel human behavior, to tell us the what, where, when, and how. The Inuit seal-eaters had a point: just as sex is a natural biological behavior that society, culture, and religion direct into culturally "acceptable" outlets, meat-eating is equally natural and normal. Few readers would accept sex as ethically wrong, even though various sects—the Koreshans of south Florida (late 1800s to early 1900s), miscellaneous nuns and priests, an array of ascetics—may have declared abstinence as the shining path. The same principle holds true of meat. Although a sect or sub-culture may abstain, the biological naturalness and normalcy of meat consumption redefines the question to one of boundaries rather than expression. It's not about *whether* eating meat is ethical, but rather *when* and *under what parameters*. And for Christians, there is clear guidance that doing so is not only allowed but good.

Cultures use a variety of environmental, religious, and cultural inputs to define if, how, and when eating animals is allowed. Take religion: devout Hindus abstain from eating cow meat; Muslims and Jews, pork. For Christians, the question was answered from Scripture: eat what you want when you please, giving thanks to God for the food. But for animal rights moralists, that view is overly simplistic if not downright exploitative, driven by an illegitimate ethical hegemony that has prevented cultures from treating animals well.

Peter Singer picked up this strain of criticism in 2002 when he noted that religion, and specifically Christianity, provides almost unassailable ethical justifications for using animals. He seemed to be saying that if God is on your side, then you are pretty much immune to extraneous ethical arguments. Then Matthew Scully located the fulcrum of Christian justifications on "dominion"—the idea that God gives people the right to use animals.[2]

But what Singer and Scully miss is that the ethical basis for animal use in the Christian tradition is richer and far more nuanced than merely ruling over animals. A central motif involves animal blood and its propitiation or atonement for transgressions—"without shedding of blood there is no forgiveness" (Hebrews 9:22). From God's animal sacrifice in the garden to cover the nakedness of Adam and Eve, to the temple sacrificial system, to the slaughter of the unblemished lamb at the Passover, the sacred text records, commands, and commends animal slaughter and infuses it with symbolic value for worshipers. Indeed, Old Testament priests were basically butchers, standing in waist-deep blood as they obeyed the commands for propitiatory sacrifices. And the eating of meat itself is deeply symbolic and worshipful: it reminds the faithful that something must die for people to live; as the meat-eater reflects on the animals' sacrifice, the meat serves as a symbol, first of the profound consequences of sin and second of the sacrifice of Christ.

Nonetheless, many activists and well-meaning omnivores are concerned: What does the Christian faith teach about eating animals and how to farm them, and what guidance does the Bible—especially the example of Jesus—provide? Are omnivores, by dint of eating animals raised in confinement for the sole purpose of human benefit, sinning against God out of ignorance or even a hardened conscience?

Basically, the animal rights movement in its modern iteration has been around at least since the 1970s. It holds to two differing but complementary views:

(a) animals have intrinsic rights by virtue of their existence, separate and distinct from people, and cannot be used by people in any way;
(b) since animals can suffer and are aware, the magnitude of suffering caused by animal agriculture cannot be justified.

However, even though the movement to protect animals has gained noted publicity and incremental victories, the number of animals slaughtered for food in the United States has increased every decade since 1970. Thus, activists faced the daunting challenge of their apparent ineffectiveness. Something—anything!—other than their own arguments had to be to blame for failure. Facing their failed efforts to convert contented omnivores dependent on industrial agriculture that supports their enjoyment of meat, animal rights intellectuals inevitably identified Christianity as a major obstacle preventing widespread cultural adoption of their animal-protection ideals.

Animal rights ideology, faced with these vestigial Christian cultural barriers like *dominion* and the *imago Dei* (image of God)—concepts discussed further in the next chapter—could only advance so far.[3] Indeed, philosophers like Peter Singer and Bernie Rollin noticed that even in a post-Christian culture that had largely forsaken its historic doctrinal moorings, people retained ideas like human exceptionalism as the rationale for animal use. Singer has lamented that many such Christian presuppositions—"Humans alone are made in the image of God" and "God gives humans dominion over the animals"—have inhibited animal liberation. The Christian tradition is "speciesist"—the arbitrary favoring of one species over the rest.

To Katie, these ideas seem as farfetched as making a silk purse out of a sow's ear, as foreign and cockamamie as time travel. How could anyone claim that meat-eating is wrong? Conversely, to Christine, the big tent of animal-protection ideology allows diverse and often divergent ideas and beliefs to cooperate in the greater cause of ending animal agriculture as we know it. Indeed, if it works toward ending animal suffering in the meat industry, why not use it?

Put another way, whether their means be the sacred or the profane, animal rights ideologues and philosophers pick and choose arguments that fit their ends of ending the consumption of meat, especially that from high-production farms. On the one hand, some of them argue that people and animals are the same; hence the same ethical standards apply to both. On the other hand, some of them argue that people really are different than animals, and that difference obligates people to take care of animals and end their suffering.

In one context, they erase the boundaries between people and animals in a type of utilitarian moral relativism that sees maximizing pleasure and minimizing pain as ultimate goods; in another, they harken to greater values outside ourselves, to a world that elevates compassion and caring to ultimate goods; and in still another, they call forth religious arguments to regulate believers' behavior. As diverse as all these arguments are, they attack the universality of meat-eating, and desire by any means possible to undermine the legitimacy of modern animal farming and meat-eating. It is to one of the most powerful of these motivations, religion—and specifically Christianity—that we now turn.

4. Joy or Grief? Understanding the Challenges to Christian Meat-Eating

WES JAMISON

"RELIGION" AND ANIMAL RIGHTS

In the previous chapter, we reviewed how meat-eating has been a (nearly) universally accepted practice for humans from the beginning. Of course, there are exceptions—some devout Hindus and Jains in particular, for example. This near-universality, however, hasn't prevented certain intellectuals from mounting various challenges to this practice.

This brings us to the matter of "religion." As the anarchist/philosopher Pierre-Joseph Proudhon noted, all political arguments are at their core religious.[1] Of course, *religion* is notoriously difficult to define. Martin Marty, noted "religion" scholar at the University of Chicago, has said that there are at least seventeen different definitions of this term and that scholars will never agree on one.[2]

Indeed, everyone has something of a "religious" fervor or dedication to his core beliefs. Every person has a "philosophy of life" or a "worldview" at whose center is a fundamental and deeply personal heart-commitment. The atheist, agnostic, or secularist holds to her views about reality, morality, and meaning as "religiously" as the Christian or Muslim. And even "secularists" or "atheists" can't simply assume their view of reality is the default position. Interestingly, the U.S. Supreme Court has adopted a functional definition of religion where the *content* of the religious beliefs is not as important as their *function*. In other words, if their beliefs function as a comprehensive guide to their lives, then even atheists can be said to have religious beliefs. Given this, the question is, What *justifies* their view? And why *their particular version* of secularism rather than another?

Some secularists say humans have value and rights, while others deny this claim. The animal rights activist is no exception.

That said, we noted in the last chapter that the animal rights movement is confronted with stalled progress in its quest to end animal exploitation. In response, they have dogmatically, and some could say "religiously," followed Singer's call:

> "I think that mainstream Christianity has been a problem for the animal movement," he told an animal rights conference at a hotel near Washington, D.C., where he also declared that conservative fundamentalists are out to create "a huge gulf between humans and animals." ... Judeo-Christian teachings that animals do not have souls, that humans were created in the image of God and are granted dominion over animals creates [sic] "a very negative influence on the way in which we think about animals," he told an audience at the Animal Rights 2002 conference, organized by a coalition of groups including People for the Ethical Treatment of Animals and the Animal Legal Defence Fund.[3]

Once philosophers and sophisticates realized the centrality of Christian freedom, they understood the necessity of attacking that freedom.

THREE CHRISTIAN DOCTRINES UNDER ASSAULT
Any understanding of their particular way of interpreting the Bible in such a way as to remove biblical permission for meat-eating and confinement farming begins with scriptural doctrines that have supported animal use in both Old Testament and New Testament times. The first doctrine that comforts the Christian who asks "Am I permitted to eat meat, even meat from big farms?" involves the idea of *dominion*. In Christian thought, dominion forms the basis for the human use and stewardship of animals. That idea emerges very early in Genesis: "And God blessed them. And God said to them, 'Be fruitful and multiply and fill the earth and subdue it, and have dominion over the fish of the sea and over the birds of the heavens and over every living thing that moves on the earth'" (Genesis 1:28, ESV).

The Hebrew word for dominion (*radah*) carries with it the idea of stewardship provided by a lord or overseer who has authority to act. In other words, God gives the right to people to use his creation—including animals—for human benefit, but not without taking into consideration the needs of the animal. But this raises the question of how people should actually treat animals and what dominion looks like in everyday practice. In other words, how should the farmers raising animals actually treat them, and how should people who eat animals view agricultural production? Importantly, the Lord's prescriptions concerning animal treatment are quite specific in some cases in the Old Testament. But in the New Testament, under the New Covenant through Christ, many of those prohibitions are explicitly overturned in favor of human freedom. Indeed, the Bible is not an animal husbandry manual. And importantly, dominion is linked to the Hebrew word *kabash*, which means to "subdue" creation through exertion and creativity. In other words, we're not only given dominion, but we're called to subdue creation, to develop it, and to form it.

Furthermore, with rare exceptions, the church has historically understood that when God was silent as revealed in the Bible, human reason and conscience guided the treatment of animals. In other words, dominion carried not only responsibility *to* God and authority *from* God but freedom *before* God.

The second core doctrine regarding farming and eating animals is *human exceptionalism*—that people are different from every other creature. As we describe in parts III and IV, the idea that people really are different is a linchpin of the entire argument for eating animals. Although humans are part of the created order, they are uniquely created in the image of God—the *imago Dei*. This includes the capacity to know and love and worship God and also to rule creation with God as vice-regents. Historically, the book of Genesis was viewed as supporting human uniqueness because only people were created in God's image, sharing certain divine attributes in limited form, such as relationality, creativity, spirituality, moral responsibility, and self-awareness. Likewise, as free agents, only people had the capacity to sin. Aristotle observed that human beings are the only "animals" with the capacity to deviate from their design and the fulfillment of their purpose. But most importantly, only people are spiritual and moral beings made to relate to God and are thus eternally accountable to him. Contrary to Peter Singer's claim, the Christian can agree with Aristotle, who said that animals, like plants, do have "souls." Walter Kaiser provides a nuanced discussion of this in chapter 7. Nonetheless, animals have an animating, self-organizing capacity that involves sensation and locomotion, but humans go beyond this with their rational capacity as well. We could add, too, that humans—unlike animals—have moral capacities as well as the ability to survive bodily death.

Third, *divine permission* in the Bible makes it clear that people may use and kill animals for human benefit. As stated before, only *some* animals were off-limits to Jews, while the production and consumption of others was not only permissible but commanded. In Genesis 15, God himself commanded Abraham to slaughter animals and cut them in half so that he might pass through the pieces. God likewise provided the substitutionary ram in the place of Abraham's sacrifice of Isaac (Genesis 22). And God himself commanded that the temple sacrifice involve the killing of animals. Indeed, the uniform biblical motif narrates that without the spilling of blood there would be no remission of sins.

In any conservative reading, the Old Testament is infused with divinely permitted or commanded bloodletting. And the sheer volume of animal sacrifices demanded by God meant that intensive livestock production systems of some type were necessary to keep up with the raw demand for animals. Joe Regenstein, professor emeritus of food science at Cornell University and a scholar of kosher and halal slaughter, estimates that the number could easily have exceeded 1.5 million animals per year.[4] This hasn't prevented some critics from questioning the ethics of large-scale farming. Philosopher John Hare notes, "We are the masters of cruelty to animals. There is nothing in ancient Israel like our factory farming, and how we treat chickens and veal calves."[5] But this ignores the historical reality of animal sacrifices in general, and the Jewish sacrifices in particular. There is simply no way the Jews could have raised and slaughtered the number of animals commanded by God without intensive agricultural practices. And the process was brutal by modern standards: indeed, Christian scholars and Jewish commentators have observed the bloody nature of the sacrificial system, noting that rabbis were basically butchers who stood in deep puddles of blood as they slaughtered the vast array of sacrificial animals required by God. Furthermore, Jewish slaughter prohibited anesthetizing the animals before killing them!

In this context, contemporary consumers who are offended by the reality of industrial processes applied to living beings seek a salve for their sensitivities and comfort for their consciences. "How," they ask, "could a loving and compassionate God allow, much less command, such barbarity?" But this ointment has more to do with the separation of death and dying from modern sensibilities—our own animals, the elderly, and soldiers die somewhere else, out of sight and out of mind—than it does with biblical mandates. Although the Old Testament sacrifices differed quantitatively from modern intensive animal slaughter, there is little qualitative difference. Hence, the isolation of modern consumers, including philosophers, activists, and academics, from the death process means that they recoil from the aesthetic shock of mass slaughter of animals. There simply is no contemporaneous witness in the early church that Christians, many of whom emerged out of the Jewish milieu, raised questions of conscience about killing and eating animals. To them, death and killing was a way of life, the consumption of animals an integral part of their worldview and cosmology.

Then, in the New Testament, the theme gains strength and clarity as Christ himself becomes the sacrifice for sins. And it is clear that in a fallen world the result of sin is death and that death cannot be eliminated except in the second coming of Christ to put in final order the new creation—the new heavens and new earth. From his eating lamb at the Passover to his provision of fish to feed people, Christ provided ample examples of killing animals. And in one instance, he clearly showed more concern for one human who had been oppressed by demonic forces than he did for the 2,000 swine that were driven off the cliff by those unclean spirits. These truths notwithstanding, given an increasing doctrinal and biblical illiteracy in evangelical churches, many Christians are not well equipped to defend those core presuppositions in a post-Christian culture.

THE FLAWS IN THE "CHRISTIAN" ANIMAL RIGHTS MOVEMENT

Furthermore, in the last few decades, animal rights philosophers and theologians agitated for a "new understanding" of the Bible that would prove advantageous to their cause. But between the 1970s and 1990s, these efforts were largely marginal to the animal welfare debate, as society grappled with defining animal abuse and dealing with egregious cases of animal mistreatment. Put simply, nobody was listening to fringe arguments that Christianity "actually taught" animal rights. But Singer's assertions concerning the Christian assumptions that allegedly hindered sweeping animal-protection victories became an alarm bell to both intellectuals and animal rights groups as they were frustrated by incremental progress at best, or seeming recidivism at worst.

In response, they turned to religion as a tool to persuade consumers of the immorality of "animal exploitation." The HSUS even opened a "Faith Outreach" effort to persuade churches and congregations of the righteousness of the new animal "hermeneutic"—the method of interpreting Scripture. Stephen Vantassel and Nelson Kloosterman astutely observe,

> Putting religion in service to the agenda of the vegetarian/animal food ethic has penetrated the fabric of Evangelicalism. This co-opting of religion, theology, and Bible-quoting in service to animal food morality is no longer restricted to some faddish cleric blessing pets in church and composing the associated litany. It has now acquired a semblance of intellectual and institutional endorsement among those presenting themselves as Bible-believing Evangelicals.[6]

As noted in chapter 3, Matthew Scully, a Roman Catholic, wrote the influential *Dominion* and popularized the idea that the traditional reading of Genesis did not support the American idea of widespread animal use. Simply put, Scully took the language that *supported* animal use, turned it upside down, and used it against Christians. He argued that since we are fellow creatures, dominion requires that we respect the creaturehood of animals. Thus, the hierarchical view of dominion was leveled, placing people and animals on the same plane and requiring people to care for animals—at some level—as equals.[7] Subtle and nuanced, his argument uses the language of dominion to relocate our stewardship responsibility *from God to animals*. Furthermore, he *removes* divine permission to freely use animals according to conscience, instead replacing it with moral guilt for doing so. Our earlier discussion of Pacific Islanders who had been converted to Christianity comes to mind.

Scully's argument is fraught with cultural bias that overlooks the practices and consciences of believers in non-Western pre-industrial culture. And it is myopic in its understanding of animal suffering—which is far from obvious to the casual reader.[8] It is nonetheless appealing exactly because it uses traditional Christian terms. In other words, Scully and others take traditional Christian doctrines and words, empty them of their historic meaning, then pour their own favorable animal protectionist meanings into the debate. This is troubling because the Christianized rhetoric of animal rights and animal welfare is targeting people who lack the understanding to refute it.

It cannot be overemphasized that animal rights groups are dedicated to redefining and co-opting Christian support for animal use. The HSUS founded its "Religion and Animals" campaign (later to become its "Faith Outreach Program") to empower theology that opposes the exploitation of animals. In other words, the "ends" are abolition, and the "means" are any theology that gets them there. Furthermore, Scully, in an apologetic distributed by HSUS, notes, "A kindly attitude toward animals is not a subjective sentiment; it is the correct moral response to the objective value of a fellow creature."[9] And the effort to reinterpret biblical freedoms and mandates regarding animal use has gained traction in traditionally Christian universities.

Christian philosophy professor Matthew Halteman makes the case for vegetarianism, claiming that "compassionate eating" can facilitate Christ's peaceable kingdom. Mirroring Scully, he argues that people are called to treat animals as fellow creatures *because* we have dominion over them. In effect, he redefines the human relationship toward animals as that of a zookeeper rather than a vice-regent with God. He also argues that God's future redemptive plan calls people to actively reflect the coming kingdom. This idea is often referred to as post-millenarianism, or the idea that Jesus established his kingdom on earth via his preaching and redemptive actions in the first century. Subsequently, he equipped the church with the gospel message, the Holy Spirit, and the Great Commission (Matthew 28:19). In effect, this belief system leads to the view that believers can "Christianize" the world and in some ways "usher in the final kingdom of God." Indeed, any reading of the Christianized theology of the animal rights movement shows a heavy reliance on Scriptures like Isaiah 11:6–7 that promise a future peaceable kingdom can happen now. And an online search for books about the "peaceable kingdom" turns up a wide assortment that take up this theme.

While not explicitly postmillennial in his theology, Halteman's appeal borders on millenarian ideals about reversing the effects of the fall. Indeed, he hints that humanity's role in the end times involves personally rejecting the creation's groaning and longing for a permanent new creation, noted in Romans 8. Breathtaking in its audacity, his argument is difficult for the Christian meat-eater to refute, exactly because it sounds so right; after all, who would be *against* the glorious redemption promised in Revelation 21 and 22? While diverging from the teachings of Christianity, he appeals to the self-righteousness of the hearers, elevating personal asceticism and pietism to an ethical "good" as people forgo their freedom to eat animals in service to a moralized diet. Indeed, Christians in a herding or hunting culture would find this reasoning rather offensive. Imagine telling an Inuit convert to become vegetarian when the only source of sustenance is animals!

These arguments generally follow a relatively predictable and inflexible track. First, they make a direct, albeit subtle, attack on human exceptionalism, in effect arguing that people are the same as animals. This stands in stark contrast to orthodox doctrine, like that in the 1561 Belgic Confession, which sees a layered and differentiated creation in service to humanity and to its Creator:

> We believe that the Father, by the Word, that is, by his Son, hath created of nothing, the heaven, the earth, and all creatures, as it seemed good unto him, giving unto every creature its being, shape, form, and several offices to serve its Creator. That he doth also still uphold and govern them by his eternal providence, and infinite power, for the service of mankind, to the end that man may serve his God. (Article 12)

The chief author of this document, Guido de Brès, was reflecting Ecclesiastes' truism that "there's nothing new under the sun." It is important to remember that the current controversy is nothing new, and de Brès and his colleagues were addressing arguments that were very similar to today's. They pointed out that humanity is special in its relationship to both God and creation—yes, God created everything, but only humanity is made in his image—and that although creation is sustained by God, *it is done so to serve humans so that humans may in turn serve God*. There, in a single statement, is a doctrinal distinction that offends animal rights theologians: there *is* a hierarchy in creation, humanity *is* special, and creation *does* serve humanity. Furthermore, rather than having responsibility *to our fellow non-human creatures*, we alone have responsibility *to a holy God from whom we draw life and to whom we owe worship*. This does not negate our stewardship responsibility to treat creation with wisdom and care, nor does it rescind the mandate to develop it, but rather shows that true stewardship includes knowing our place in the created order and making the important human-nonhuman distinction between earthly creatures. And, in this, we are guided by conscience when the Scripture is silent. In other words, we have great freedom when it comes to raising, using, slaughtering, and consuming animals.

While animal rights groups and moralists strive to reframe *dominion* and the *imago Dei*, Vantassel and Kloosterman rightly argue that this heterodox theology uses familiar Christian language, replacing its original meaning with an entirely different meaning. They critique Halteman's position, showing how he misappropriates Bible verses through proof-texting and quoting passages without context. They conclude that Halteman selectively quotes Scripture to forward the cause of animal rights more than the cause of Christ. Similarly, they argue that Halteman arbitrarily uses Scripture to make his case. Nowhere does Halteman mention where God causes death or commands it, as in the garden of Eden to cover Adam and Eve (Genesis 3:21) or the temple sacrifice. Nor does he mention where Jesus himself speaks of celebrating the prodigal son's return with feasting on the fatted calf or where he cooks fish for his disciples. And Jesus, being a good Jew and living under the Mosaic Law, would have certainly partaken of the lamb at Passover.

Upon examination, arguments by Halteman and others are revealed as faulty in their theology and their logic and in the abuse of secondary sources. Even Christian lay farmers without theological education notice the inconsistency when he specifically targets industrial agriculture as the culprit of abuse without addressing whether and under what circumstances eating animals from "compassionate" farms would be acceptable. Instead, he seems to argue that death itself is the offense. In his worldview, Christians are to remove personal culpability for causing the death of animals from their lives.

Finally, when Halteman quotes the church father St. Basil because he purportedly venerated creation and animals, the quotation comes from a source that does not exist. Here is part of it (paraphrased): "enlarge within us the sense of fellowship with all living things, our little brothers, to whom thou hast given this earth as their home in common with us."[10] This spurious source espouses a fictitious theology: the fact that animals are fellow creatures does not thereby elevate them to the status of brothers and sisters of humans.

Vantassel and Kloosterman wryly note that

The problem, however, is that this prayer cannot be found anywhere in the writings of St. Basil of Caesarea, although several have mistakenly ascribed it to the Liturgy of St. Basil. This appeal to Basil attempts to place historic Christianity in service to the new food morality, but is little more than a vegetarian legend. It has no basis in historical fact, and yet has migrated even into The Encyclopedia of Applied Animal Behaviour and Welfare, based solely on a secondary source.[11]

CONCLUDING REMARKS

So, the bottom line is this: the new animal-protection theology overlooks divine mandates for animal slaughter, and animal rights pragmatists misappropriate Scripture in service to their agenda, misquoting or taking verses out of context; they arbitrarily proof-text Scripture, making selective use of the Bible while overlooking the clear teachings that humans may joyfully use and eat animals; and they use faulty logic and abuse secondary sources.

In the face of such sophisticated arguments, well-intended Christians may well ask, "What is the correct view of animals, and how should I act toward them?" First, humans are unique in that only they are created in the image of God. This is the non-negotiable continental divide in the animal rights debate. As theologian Harold Brown noted years ago, animal rights at its core is a rejection of human exceptionalism.[12] The *imago Dei* starkly declares the special nature of humans and their special relationship to God.

Second, although all creation was good, humanity was given a special place and power within creation in relationship to God. As the Belgic Confession so beautifully reminds us, all of creation is intended to serve humans, so that they may in turn serve God. In the wisdom of God, his creation, although stratified and hierarchical, is focused upon him and his glory. The animals serve humans, enabling them to serve and worship God. Importantly, this truth is independent of the effects of sin. Put another way, just because sinful humans abuse animals *doesn't mean* that the use of animals itself is abuse or that humans should not use them.

Similarly, Christians are reminded that since the fall, something must die for them to live. Indeed, in the Bible the creation itself was pronounced as good, after which only with the creation of people as the pinnacle of creation was everything that God made called "very good." Importantly, even though creation was called "very good," it was still transitory and incomplete; it awaits the new creation of a transformed realm of nature—including our own immortal resurrection bodies (Psalm 102:25–27; Romans 8:20–22). The Bible is filled with descriptions of the necessity of death: from the killing of animals for food and as a blood sacrifice, to the New Testament commands and permissions given to eat meat (Acts 10:12–25; Romans 14:2), to the example of Christ himself, who ate animals, killed them, and gave them to others to eat (Luke 24:42; John 6:11; 21:9).

Perhaps more importantly for Christians seeking to know whether, how, and when they can eat meat, believers are given warnings about being watchful about ascetics and false teachers who place them under dietary restrictions:

> Now the Spirit expressly says that in later times some will depart from the faith by devoting themselves to deceitful spirits and teachings of demons, through the insincerity of liars whose consciences are seared, who forbid marriage and require abstinence from foods that God created to be received with thanksgiving by those who believe and know the truth. For everything created by God is good, and nothing is to be rejected if it is received with thanksgiving, for it is made holy by the word of God and prayer. (1 Timothy 4:1–5, ESV)

Indeed, elsewhere Paul says that it is the *weak* in faith (i.e., in conscience) who believe they should be vegetarian (Romans 14:2)! So mature believers who understand their freedom in Christ can use animals and eat them with joy and thanksgiving.

When all is said and done, believers are responsible to God for how they worship him. All of creation is given to humankind to use, but not for its own purposes alone. All that humanity is, has, and does is provided by God so that the believer can in turn bring glory to him. That includes sustenance from creation, and that sustenance includes animals. Rather than submit their consciences to those who are offended by the images of farming and slaughter, believers can rest in the knowledge that a good and gracious God lovingly provides them with meat to eat and the processes and technologies that produces those animals.

Once, while I sat with Indian Christians in Chennai during a Bible study, they served a curry dish filled with chicken meat. Having been converted from Hinduism, they knew well the concept of religious abstinence from meat, and they rejected it with the joy and freedom that only Christ brings. And they recognized that the dead animals they were eating served as an allegory of the sacrifice of Christ: with a smile, they said, "something has to die for us to live," and without malice or guilt, they gratefully consumed the meat set before them.

So the advice to Katie (from chapter 3) is this: "Keep doing what you're doing, making the best BBQ pork and beef from pigs and cows raised in intensive agriculture systems, all the while giving thanks for it to the loving God who makes provision for sin." And the advice to Christine, like the apostle Paul's admonition in Romans 14, is to follow your conscience while allowing others to do the same, and realize that your convictions are not others' commands.

So, Christian, eat, give thanks, and rejoice in the Lord's goodness!

PART III
WHY PEOPLE MATTER

5. There Is Nothing Morally Wrong with Eating Meat

TIMOTHY HSIAO

The animal rights movement loudly and boldly proclaims that meat consumption is grossly immoral.[1] For defenders of animal rights, the decision to go vegan isn't merely a matter of one's personal lifestyle choices; it is a direct moral obligation that is binding upon all of us.

In defense of this position, pro-vegan ethicists have deployed a number of philosophical arguments that purport to show that animals have serious moral status and that both meat consumption and modern animal agricultural practices violate this status.[2] The goal of this chapter is to respond to these arguments and make the case for the moral permissibility of eating meat. My arguments do not rely on any particular set of theological assumptions. Although I am a Christian who believes that Scripture permits meat-eating, I argue that meat-eating can be justified philosophically apart from appealing to divine revelation.[3]

A FRAMEWORK FOR RIGHTS AND MORAL STATUS

Before we can resolve the question of whether animals have rights or serious moral status, we first need to establish a framework for understanding what these concepts mean, what they refer to, and how they are justified.[4] Much of the debate over the morality of eating meat hinges on fundamental questions surrounding the nature of rights, personhood, and morality itself. So let's first turn to these issues.

All major moral theories agree that morality is fundamentally about the pursuit of what is good and the avoidance of what is evil. Whatever else we may say about its various nuances, this seems to be the core of what morality is. The whole point of morality, moral theorizing, and moral living is so that we may *be* moral—that is, to determine the truth about the good life so that it may be pursued through activity. Philosophers may disagree over *what* good and evil are, but *that* they are to be respectively pursued and avoided is something on which they can all agree.

Morality, then, is fundamentally about a certain type of *action*—namely, action in pursuit of what is good and action in avoidance of what is evil. Action of this kind, however, requires *knowledge* of what is good and what is evil, for one cannot act to pursue good and avoid evil if one does not know what good and evil are. Thus, the two fundamental objects of morality are knowledge and action.[5]

Since morality is about action in pursuit of the good, it follows that membership in the moral community requires that a being be capable of (a) knowing what is good and evil and (b) acting for the sake of that knowledge. Whether the moral life consists of fulfilling duties, maximizing utility, or developing certain character dispositions, morality as such is something that can only be articulated, understood, and practiced by *rational beings.*

Accordingly, a being has *moral status* only if it possesses a rational nature.[6] Now if something has moral status, then there is a strong moral presumption against harming or killing it.[7] In other words, beings with moral status are owed respect and justice on our part. This is best understood in terms of *rights*. A being with moral status has the moral *right* to be given fair and equal treatment and the moral *right* to be allowed to act in ways that promote its well-being.

We can think of a *moral right* as a claim or entitlement to some good or service. To have a right is to have the moral authority to do something or to have something provided to you. Rights impose corresponding obligations on others to respect them, be it through non-interference or by providing their bearers with something. For example, if I have the right to demand payment from you, then you have the obligation to pay me. If I have the right to bodily integrity, you have the moral obligation not to interfere with my well-being. The function of a right is thus to *protect* certain goods that its bearer needs to thrive. In the words of one philosopher, rights are "moral shields."[8]

Now it is a self-evident truth that we as human beings have rights.[9] But *why* do we have them? Recall that the fundamental principle of morality is that good should be done and evil should be avoided. This task cannot be accomplished unless we are afforded some degree of protection as we go about pursuing the moral life. This is where rights enter into the equation. Rights exist to guard the things that we need in order to go about fulfilling our duties. They give us the "moral space" necessary to do what morality demands of us. Thus, I have the rights to life and bodily integrity because they are prerequisites to any meaningful pursuit of the good. I have the right to freedom of expression because I have the obligation to develop my talents.

In other words, rights protect things that are morally valuable, and something is morally valuable if it contributes towards the fulfillment of morality's purpose, which is the pursuit of what is good and the avoidance of what is evil. Accordingly, only rational beings can have rights, for only rational beings are capable of knowing what is good and acting for that reason.

WHY ANIMALS LACK MORAL STATUS

Animals lack moral status because they are incapable of having duties, and they are incapable of having duties because they lack the kind of rationality necessary to act for moral reasons.

None of this is to say that animals are completely unintelligent or devoid of creative behavior. On the contrary, many animals are capable of amazing behavior. Rather, the point is that whatever kind of intelligence animals do have, it is not the type of intelligence relevant to being a moral subject.[10] Knowledge of what is good requires that one be capable of understanding what is fulfilling for oneself and others, and hence a moral subject must have a mind capable of grasping the nature or essence of things—what is sometimes called the *agent intellect*. Despite all the complex behaviors demonstrated by many species of animals, none comes close to demonstrating this capacity.[11]

We come to know what something is through observing its actions. That is, we know what kind of being something is by seeing how its powers, capacities, and dispositions are manifested. I know what a plant is by observing its physical structure and growth patterns. I know what a dog is by observing its behavior. If some animals really were capable of rational agency, then they would have an intellect like ours. If that were the case, then we should expect them to manifest some of the characteristics indicative of it. But any evidence of this sort is completely absent in animals. This can be seen simply by noting the huge gaps in achievements between humans and animals. Our nature as rational agents has provided us with the basis for the intellectual and technological achievements typical to human civilization. If animals possessed the same sort of intelligence, then we would expect to see similar achievements in the animal world. We would expect their intellectual, moral, social, and cultural development to parallel our own. Yet this is obviously not the case. All this is evidence that animals lack a rational nature.

Indeed, if animals *were* rational in the sense required to be a moral subject, then they would be under moral duties to each other. The cheetah would have a moral duty not to hunt the gazelle. Owls would be under a moral duty not to kill mice. Not only that, but we would be under obligations to prevent animals (who cannot help themselves) from killing each other. All of this is absurd. We do not hold animals morally responsible or put them on trial for their apparent misdeeds. Animals kill and maim each other, but there is no moral significance to these actions.

However, some defenders of animal rights argue that even if animals don't have rights, they still must surely possess *some* degree of moral status because they are able to feel pain.[12] They argue that as long as animals can suffer, they have some moral worth. In that case, there is still room to carve out a minimalist argument for moral veganism on the basis of unjustified pain.[13]

This doesn't work. The capacity to feel pain is the capacity to have a certain kind of experience. But what matters for moral status isn't the ability to have experiences; rather it is the capacity to know what is good and pursue it. A being that is able to feel pain will have a richer experiential life than a being that lacks this ability, but unless it is capable of acting for moral reasons, it cannot count as a member of the moral community. The capacity to feel pain *by itself* does not give a being this crucial ability.

So why do pro-vegan philosophers think that pain has inherent moral significance? The answer that's typically offered is that pain is by definition a *bad* thing. I don't like pain, and neither do you. We are *harmed* when we suffer. Our well-being is diminished. The same is true of animals. So pain matters for them as much as it does for us, right?

No. While it is true that *our* pain experiences have moral significance, we cannot infer from this that pain *itself* is morally significant for merely *any* creature that experiences pain. Simply because an entity's well-being or proper functioning has been disrupted, this by itself isn't morally significant. Consider this: it is disruptive to a tree's proper function ("bad") that I cut it down and turn it into a chair. Those actions *harm* the integrity of the tree and diminish its well-being. Of course, the tree is totally incapable of feeling pain, but there are plenty of other ways in which something "bad" can befall it. This is true of other things as well. If your computer becomes infected with a virus, then something *"bad"* has happened to it. If your car's engine overheats and breaks down, then something *"bad"* has happened to your car. In none of these cases does the mere presence of a measure of harm or disruption ("badness") confer any kind of moral status to the entities in question. So the mere capacity to feel pain cannot have inherent moral significance for animals simply because it represents a measure of well-being. That is, whatever interrupts an entity's proper function doesn't thereby translate to moral badness; otherwise, trees, computers, and cars would also have moral status and rights.

Here's another way of looking at it: Pain is bad (i.e., disruptive) for animals. Likewise, logging is bad for trees and magnets are bad for computers. What makes all of these things bad is the *same feature*: namely, that an entity's well-being or proper functioning has been disrupted. Now the fact that pain provides a measure of badness (i.e., disruption to proper function) can't be what confers moral status, for otherwise trees and computers would also have moral standing on account of there being ways in which their well-being can be impaired.

What this all shows is that there is really nothing *special* about pain as far as badness and harm are concerned. *Our* pain experiences are morally significant because they occur within the context of beings who are capable of rational and moral deliberation. Outside of that context, however, pain experiences do not have any inherent moral significance. It should be emphasized that I am *not* saying that animals cannot feel pain. Of course they can, although the extent to which they are aware of pain has been questioned.[14] My point is simply that their pain experiences are not morally significant in themselves.

This is not to say that we can cause pain to animals willy-nilly. We may not have duties directly to animals in respect of their well-being, but we do have duties to ourselves and each other that require us to respect animal welfare. We may not inflict pointless pain ("torture" and "abuse") or otherwise mistreat animals, for in doing so we corrupt our own character, which also disposes us towards cruelty against our fellow humans.

THE ARGUMENT FROM "MARGINAL CASES"

Perhaps the most common argument against any attempt to deny moral status to animals is the *argument from marginal cases*.[15] We can summarize the argument as follows: If animals lack moral status because they cannot reason, then newborns, infants, and those who are mentally disabled must also lack moral status. But since newborns, infants, and the mentally disabled do have moral status in spite of their inability to reason, the ability to reason is not necessary for moral status.

This argument easily fails. The response is simply that all humans, regardless of age or disability, have moral status because they possess a *rational nature*. That is, all humans, in virtue of being the *kind* of organism they are, possess a basic or root capacity to reason.[16] This capacity may be immature, undeveloped, or impeded in the case of certain individuals, but this does not entail that the capacity is non-existent.[17] What is lacking in so-called marginal cases is not the capacity to reason but its *manifestation*.

Consider a rock and a human being who is born without eyes. Both lack the ability to see, yet the human being's lack of sight is deficient in a way that the rock's lack of sight is not. This is because human beings, unlike rocks, *ought* to see. There is an inherent normativity in the human ability to see that is not present in the rock. What explains this normativity is the fact that all humans as such have root powers and capacities oriented towards fulfillment. Without appeal to the normativity provided by these capacities, we would have no basis for our concepts of well-being, flourishing, maturity, immaturity, defectiveness, or disability. These capacities provide a benchmark by which we can evaluate whether a thing's life is going well or ill.

Root capacities are also what guide the growth, development, and proper functioning of an individual and hence are present from the moment an individual begins to exist. Human embryos, for instance, develop in the way they do because their growth is inherently directed from within by their nature. An embryo's root capacities function as a blueprint that dictates how the process of biological development should proceed. The root capacity to reason is no different. The reason why normal adult humans have the mature capacity to reason is because we have a root capacity to reason that directs our development towards maturation. Since this root capacity is what guides our development, it is present in us from the very beginning of our existence. Thus, *all* human beings, from conception to death, have moral status because they possess this rational nature throughout every moment of their lives.[18] This is true even if their development is impeded or if they never develop the physical organs necessary to express their rational capacities. There are simply no such things as marginal cases.[19]

"YOU WOULDN'T EAT A DOG!"

Some argue that there are glaring inconsistencies in the way we regard animals that are dear to us compared to those killed for consumption, and that these inconsistencies can be leveraged into an argument against meat-eating. One of People for the Ethical Treatment of Animals (PETA's) campaigns, for example, depicts a series of animals and challenges viewers to draw the line on where it is acceptable to eat them, with the implication being that any line we draw is arbitrary. PETA's point is that there are no morally relevant differences between the animals we value and the animals we consume. So, if it is wrong to eat a dog or cat, then is also wrong to eat a cow or chicken. Many vegan street activists have incorporated this argumentative strategy into their outreach efforts, and at least one philosopher has attempted to turn it into a serious moral argument.[20]

I fail to see how this argument is even remotely convincing. Take the practice of using dogs and cats as food. Such a practice strikes many in

Western society as disgusting, sickening, and inhumane. But why? The explanation is likely due to the fact that dogs are regarded as companion animals with special social value. Individuals in Western cultures have, through various social practices, conferred "honorary moral standing" to dogs and cats in virtue of the roles that they have set for them. We relate to our pets in ways similar to how we relate with human beings. For many of us, dogs occupy the role of an honorary family member.

Hence, mistreating an animal that is regarded as a companion is good evidence of a cruel disposition, which also explains why the practice of eating a dog in the United States is bound up with a certain kind of social stigma. But while dogs have been accorded this special social value, chickens, cows, pigs, and other animals commonly farmed on an industrial level have not. This explains why many people feel the way they do when confronted with the prospect of consuming dogs but not other animals. So we cannot generalize from our revulsion towards the slaughter of dogs to the slaughter of cows or chickens. The disgust we associate with eating dogs can be adequately explained without having to attribute moral status to them.

This is not to appeal to some crude form of moral relativism but to acknowledge the fact that while animals lack moral standing, our attitudes towards them are shaped not just by our sympathy towards them but also by the ways in which we use them. Thus, our intuition that there is something revolting about eating dogs but not other animals is defensible.

Moreover, the fact that dogs have special social value is a contingent association. There is nothing intrinsically wrong with eating dogs, as strange or disgusting as it may seem to us. In societies where dogs and cats are not thought of in the way that we think of them—such as in some Asian cultures—there is no association of cruelty or disgust in eating them. Observers outside of these cultures may recoil in disgust, but such a reaction is simply a reflection of the special social value that dogs have within their own society.[21]

Consider the consumption of cows, which is commonplace in Western society but frowned upon in India, where some states have completely banned the slaughter of cows due to their religious significance. Many Indians would regard the slaughter of cows in much the same way as Americans regard the eating of dogs. But strictly speaking, there is *no real difference* between eating a dog and eating a cow (except, perhaps, the taste). If it is morally permissible to eat one, then it is morally permissible to eat the other. Animal rights advocates are correct when they point out that there is no *fundamental* difference between the animals we keep as companions and the animals we consume. But this isn't a strike against the view I am defending. Rather, it is an honest acknowledgment that we value animals differently depending on the purposes we have for them. Understood this way, there is nothing morally arbitrary in being willing to gobble down a turkey while also being squeamish about eating a dog or cat.

WHAT ABOUT FACTORY FARMING?

Even if eating meat is morally permissible in principle, might some of our current practices still nevertheless be unjustified? Many critics of animal rights nevertheless condemn factory farming as cruel and depraved. However, I think there is a case to be made in defense of our modern agricultural practices.

As a definition of animal cruelty, we may say that an act is cruel if it reveals a corrupt character or if it corrupts one's character so as to make one more disposed to mistreating humans. Both animals and humans experience pain. As we saw in the previous chapter, the human capacity for pain often involves the moral dimension, but this is not so for animals, which are not moral beings. Even so, to inflict pointless pain on animals, to inflict pain for the sake of causing pain, or to cause pain for sheer amusement is not only an abuse of our stewardship over creation, but such an act disposes one towards similar behavior when it comes to human suffering. But there is no straightforward way to give a catch-all list of the practices that meet the criteria of what some would consider "cruelty" to animals. Since animals lack moral status, what some may count as a cruel practice towards animals will turn out to be person-specific. A practice that evinces a cruel character for one person may not be considered cruel for another. John Smith may be able to work in a slaughterhouse for his entire life without there being anything amiss about his character, while the same profession may allow Hannibal Lecter an outlet to cultivate his sadism. Hence we cannot in any way issue a unilateral condemnation of this-or-that practice (much less the *entire* industrial farming industry) as being cruel.

A practice like high density confinement may appear shocking to those who are especially sympathetic to animals or who have lived in a largely urbanized society in which direct contact with animals is limited mainly to pets. But for those who work with animals daily, there need not be anything cruel about this. Confinement, branding, clipping, force-feeding, and other practices found in concentrated animal feeding operations (CAFOs) are not there for their own sake but are understood as part of a trade with a morally significant purpose: human well-being. So long as this point is kept in mind, those who carry out these practices can do so with the goal of promoting human well-being and not to enjoy harming animals for the sake of harming animals. Industrial animal agriculture may involve some rather graphic details, but to say that it is inherently cruel in the sense outlined earlier is false.

Warfare provides a very helpful analogy to the point I am trying to make. Participating in combat isn't pretty, to say the least. War can be a very traumatic experience for certain individuals. Soldiers may go insane, lose their sense of human dignity, or turn into cold-blooded killers. For these persons, being a soldier may very well be morally hazardous (which is why the military is careful to administer psychological evaluations). But while being a soldier is certainly a risky activity—one that not everyone is cut out for—it does not entail the development of a cruel disposition. Soldiers can fight virtuously, honorably, and even show love for their enemies while on the battlefield.[22] An outside observer who looks at the horrors of war (or law enforcement, for that matter) from a society where war or violence is unheard of may, like the critic of industrial farming, find it very hard to believe that warfare can be fought justifiably or honorably, but this is no slight against the truth that it can. Our best evidence that war can be fought honorably comes from the soldiers who do so. Likewise, our best evidence that industrial farming can be conducted humanely comes from the industrial farmers who do so.

The temptation is to look at certain practices and make sweeping generalizations based on one's own emotional revulsion: "But look at the way they are treating those chicks! How can anyone do this with a clear conscience?" Well, it is an empirical fact that many people *are* in fact able to work in animal agriculture with a clear conscience, just like many are able to fight in war and preserve their moral integrity. On the other hand, certain people are indeed corrupted. This only shows that we need to be careful in high-risk professions.

I am not denying that there are psychological costs associated with working in animal agriculture. Having to kill, skin, and butcher an animal can be traumatizing for some people. Some who work in the animal industry may very well develop cruel tendencies. All this shows is that working in animal agriculture—like participating in warfare—has moral hazards that must be carefully avoided. Being a soldier is not for everyone. Neither is being a butcher. But as for the activity of killing animals for consumption, even on the scale of industrial farms, I see no reason to think that is it inherently corrupting or cruel.

CONCLUSION

Morality is about pursuing what is good and avoiding what is evil. Thus, in order to count as a member of the moral community, a being must be capable of acting for moral reasons. All human beings meet this requirement. But animals do not, for reasons I have considered. So, we may conclude that animals lack moral standing. Accordingly, it is permissible to kill and consume them, even on the industrial level.

Much more could be written on this topic, but there's only so much that can be said in the span of a short chapter.[23] That said, the arguments given here should provide plenty of material to counter the moral case for veganism.

6. Human Lives Matter:
Reflections on Human Exceptionalism
TIMOTHY HSIAO

"What a piece of work is a man! How noble in reason,
how infinite in faculty! In form and moving how express and
admirable! In action how like an angel, in apprehension how
like a god! The beauty of the world. The paragon of animals."
(Shakespeare, *Hamlet*, Act II, scene 2)

Then God said, "Let us make man in our image, after our
likeness. And let them have dominion over the fish of the sea
and over the birds of the heavens and over the livestock
and over all the earth and over every creeping thing
that creeps on the earth."
(Genesis 1:26, ESV)

WHAT HAPPENED TO HUMAN EXCEPTIONALISM?

I teach ethics for a living. During every semester for the past few years, I have posed the following scenario to my freshman and sophomore students:

Imagine that you are standing in front of a lake. On one side, your dog is drowning. On the other side, a total stranger is also drowning. Unless something is done, they will die. You are physically fit and able to engage in a rescue. However, the circumstances dictate that you can only save one. Which one do you save?

In my mind, the answer is *blindingly obvious*: you have a clear moral obligation to save the stranger. This shouldn't even be up for debate. Yet consistently the majority of my students (around 60 to 70 percent) have answered that they would rather save their *dog*! I then modify the scenario slightly to replace the stranger with one of their classmates. Although the percentage decreases dramatically, there often still remains a sizable minority who would *let their classmate drown* and instead save their dog.[1]

I wish I could say that these responses were limited to my own informal surveys of students in introductory philosophy classes. Unfortunately, they're not. A 2013 paper published in the journal *Anthrozoös* found that an alarming 40 percent of respondents said they would save their own pet over a foreign tourist.[2] Most of the respondents who chose to save their pet explained their decision in terms of the strong emotional bond that they shared with their pets ("I love my pet" and "My pet is a part of my family"). The fact that the foreign tourist is a *human being* apparently didn't matter all that much to them.

If all this doesn't trouble you, it should. Our culture has overhumanized animals in a way that has corrupted our basic moral sensibilities. Consider the way in which many millennials have substituted pet ownership in place of having a spouse or raising children.[3] Indeed, many of them refer to their pets as their "children" and treat them as though they are human. It is not surprising, then, that many form strong attachments to their companion animals. Apparently, we've gotten so good at anthropomorphizing our pets that many people are actually starting to believe that they really are on par with humans.

All this is just a symptom of a broader problem—namely, our culture's tendency to prioritize emotions, feelings, and subjectivity over reason, objectivity, and truth.[4] We have affirmed the value of individual experience to the point where we have lost sight of crucial truths that were, until fairly recently, considered articles of common sense. One of these truths is the idea that human beings are unique and occupy a special place in nature that is above plants and animals—what is sometimes called *human exceptionalism*.

A large part of our belief system is influenced (both explicitly and implicitly) by prevailing cultural attitudes. When one's culture practically worships at the altar of feelings and experiences, it is not difficult to see how this mindset can lead to a grossly inflated view of the significance of animals. After all, animals are cute. We relate to them easily. They make us happy, evoke strong feelings of sympathy, become our companions, and create a sense of attachment. These are all wonderful things about animals that should be enjoyed, but when combined with a strong cultural emphasis on personal sentiments, it is not surprising that many individuals have erroneously humanized animals. This tendency usually develops at a young age. As philosopher Peter Carruthers points out,

In previous eras ... [c]hildren would have observed adults interacting with animals in the context of hunting, fishing, and farming (as well as listening to adults talk). However, in our own culture there are few opportunities for such correction to take place, except in respect of adults' treatment of household and garden pests (which are insects, for the most part). Most children today have no experience of hunting, and little experience of farming beyond visits to a petting zoo and whatever they learn from television and books. Most children's only contact with vertebrate animals is with pets, who are generally treated in our culture as honorary members of a family. With nothing to prevent them from doing so, children's natural inclinations to feel warmly toward people who are kind, and not unkind, to other agents, leaves them wide open to a tendency to *moralize* such feelings, resulting in a belief in the moral standing of vertebrate animals.[5]

Another reason why many have such an inflated view of animal significance owes to the way in which our culture depicts animals. Talking animals that look like humans and behave like humans feature prominently in popular entertainment. All this strikes *us* as obviously fictional, but for young children with extremely active fantasy lives, this can inflate their view of animals. As Carruthers again notes,

By overhumanizing the psychological states of animals in the fantasy lives of young people we create a tendency (which mostly remains unconscious, no doubt) to think of them as rational agents and potential collaborators, and hence as possessing moral standing in their own right.[6]

I am by no means saying that cartoons, TV shows, movies, and books that attribute human features to animals are corrupting our children. Far from it—they are enjoyable forms of entertainment! Rather, the claim is that the heightened emphasis on sentiments and human-like psychological states can dispose children to form erroneous beliefs about the moral status of animals. This is not a problem if children are taught (as they historically were) to understand the moral significance of the differences between humans and animals. Proper moral education can easily do this, but the problem is that proper moral education is difficult when the same cultural attitude that emphasizes personal sentiments also de-emphasizes the importance of reason, objectivity, and truth. Because proper moral education relies on all three of these things, their de-emphasis makes it even more difficult for children to be steered in the right direction, especially when those responsible for their instruction don't care much themselves for these things.

When individuals *do* make decisions using their rational system instead of their emotions, they will tend to prioritize what is true and rational over what they feel to be right. In the *Anthrozoös* study mentioned earlier, the overwhelming majority of those who chose to save the tourist over their pet explained their decision in terms of reasons that had nothing to do with emotions and more to do with theoretical beliefs about the significance of human life ("Human life is more valuable than animals," "God gave us dominion over animals"). The researchers noted that the "data support the notion that the decision to save human life was controlled by the 'cold' rational system and the decision to save a pet was emotionally laden."[7]

All this is unsurprising. It reveals that a renewed commitment to reason, objectivity, and truth is crucial if we want to correct the creeping moral corruption in our culture—not just with animals, but with a plethora of issues. But before this can be done, we need to know *why* humans are exceptional in a way that sets them apart from animals. Many people who believe in human exceptionalism are unable to articulate their reasons for holding this belief.[8] The next section makes the philosophical case for human exceptionalism.

IN DEFENSE OF HUMAN EXCEPTIONALISM

While we might forgive popular culture for unintentionally overhumanizing animals, there is a real, deliberate, and sustained war on humans going on within academic circles.[9] This anti-human crusade often takes the form of a wolf in sheep's clothing. Under the innocent guise of "broadening the moral community," philosophers who demand that we recognize moral standing for animals simultaneously dismiss the rights of the most vulnerable human beings. In doing so, they are not really broadening the moral community but *replacing* human beings with animals. In attempting to make morality appear more "inclusive," these philosophers exclude the humans most in need of its protection.

Consider two examples. Jeff McMahan, White's Professor of Moral Philosophy at the University of Oxford, argues that our duties to eliminate suffering in animals are so strong that we have a moral duty to intervene in nature and stop animals from preying on each other.[10] Yet, McMahan also argues that *infanticide*—the practice of killing infants after birth—is morally permissible.[11] The sympathy that is extended to mere animals, it seems, does not apply to human beings at the earliest stages of life. Along similar lines, Peter Singer, Ira W. DeCamp Professor of Bioethics at Princeton University, has argued essentially that the lives of cognitively disabled human beings are of less value than pigs.[12] Singer, who also happens to agree with McMahan about the permissibility of infanticide, has built something of a reputation for defending positions that many would regard as morally repugnant. As one critic put it, Singer and his ilk never target anybody who can fight back.

If there's any redeeming quality about McMahan, Singer, and other philosophers of their stripe, it's the fact that they are consistent with their belief system. Given the moral and scientific assumptions from which they begin, we can hardly fault them for arriving at the conclusion they do. They are simply following a worldview to its logical consequences.

And what is this worldview? Let's start with the scientific assumptions behind the modern animal rights movement. We can sum up these assumptions under the banner of naturalistic Darwinism—an evolution without any divine involvement or guidance. Proponents of animal rights argue that if this Darwinian account of evolution is true, then the idea that human beings are categorically distinct from animals is a myth. Why? Because all organisms evolved gradually through incremental changes, where organisms of one sort gave rise to organisms of another sort. Accordingly, all organisms exist on a continuum. There is no such thing as a distinct animal nature or a distinct human nature. The difference between human beings and animals is therefore only a matter of *degree*, not one of kind.[13]

The moral, social, and political implications of Darwin's theory are far-reaching. As philosopher James Rachels argues in his book *Created from Animals: The Moral Implications of Darwinism*, Darwin's theory left no room for affirming humanity as unique among animals. There is nothing particularly special about us that sets us apart from the rest of the world. We're just another kind of advanced animal. To be sure, there are *differences* between humans and other animals, but these differences are not *morally significant*. Since many of our current beliefs and practices rely on the truth of human exceptionalism, Darwinism calls for a radical revision of the way we understand morality, society, and politics. As Rachels notes,

> Darwin's theory does undermine traditional values. In particular, it undermines the traditional idea that human life has a special, unique worth ... Darwinism undermines both the idea that man is made in the image of God and the idea that man is a uniquely rational being. Furthermore, if Darwinism is correct, it is unlikely that any other support for the idea of human dignity will be found. The idea of human dignity turns out, therefore, to be the moral effluvium of a discredited metaphysics.[14]

Claims about "human nature" and "human uniqueness" have no place in a Darwinian worldview. Anything based on these ideas must either change or be scrapped completely. This includes the concept of human dignity. Thus, philosopher of science David Hull notes,

> If species evolve in anything like the way that Darwin thought they did, then they cannot possibly have the sort of natures that traditional philosophers claimed they did. If species in general lack natures, then so does *Homo Sapiens* as a biological species. If *Homo Sapiens* lacks a nature, then no reference to biology can be made to support one's claims about 'human nature' ... Because so many moral, ethical, and political theories depend on some notion or other of human nature, Darwin's theory brought into question all these theories.[15]

Nevertheless, the belief in human dignity and human uniqueness refuses to die. Perhaps recognizing its importance, some Darwinists desperately try to carve out conceptual space for affirming human uniqueness, even if it means relegating it to the realm of biological mystery:

- E. O. Wilson (biologist): "Man has intensified these vertebrate traits while adding unique qualities of his own. In so doing he has achieved an extraordinary degree of cooperation with little or no sacrifice of personal survival and reproduction. Exactly how he alone has been able to cross to this fourth pinnacle [of altruism, cooperation—without diminishing capacity for survival], reversing the downward trend of social evolution in general, is the culminating mystery of all biology."[16]
- Richard Dawkins (zoologist): "We have the power to defy the selfish genes of our birth ... We can even discuss ways of deliberately cultivating and nurturing pure, disinterested altruism—something that has no place in nature, something that has never existed before in the whole history of the world ... We, alone on earth, can rebel against the tyranny of the selfish replicators."[17]
- Daniel Dennett (philosopher): "Like other animals, we have built-in desires to reproduce and to do pretty much whatever it takes to achieve this goal ... But we also have creeds, and the ability to transcend our genetic imperatives. This fact makes us different."[18]

But why should the ability to rebel against nature be morally significant? For these individuals, nature is a "blind watchmaker" that is devoid of moral agency or value in the first place.[19] Despite their well-intentioned attempts to salvage some semblance of human dignity and human uniqueness, they amount to nothing more than extremely watered-down replacements framed in poetic language.

What then should we say about Darwinism? Must we abandon human uniqueness as outdated? Two responses are possible. First, we might say that Darwin and his followers are just flat-out wrong in their scientific claims about evolution. A second response is to say that even if Darwinians are correct about evolution, they are mistaken about its implications for human uniqueness. Both approaches have merit. While I'm skeptical of evolutionary theory, there's not enough room for me to lay out my cards in such a short chapter.[20] So, I'll take the second approach.[21]

Suppose we grant the truth of evolution. Why should we think that this rules out human uniqueness? *By itself*, it is hard to see how mere descent with modification shows that there is no categorical difference between humans and animals. At best, it only shows that there is no *biological* difference. But just because there are no biological differences does not mean that there are no differences at all. We might think that the difference between human and animals consists of something immaterial or conceptual (such as the kind of mind they possess). From a theological point of view, perhaps God at some point "refurbished" a pair or group of organisms (*hominids*). What if God directly endowed them with certain moral, volitional, and spiritual capacities that their immediate genetic predecessors did not have? This kind of event isn't the sort of thing that science could begin to verify. At any rate, the idea that humans and animals are exhausted by their physical parts is not something that science can actually show. It is, rather, a *philosophical* approach to the nature of reality.

It is only when we combine evolution through natural selection with *materialism* (i.e., the view that matter is all the reality there is) that we reach the conclusion that there is no categorical difference between human beings and animals. But again, materialism is not a scientific doctrine; nor can it be demonstrated by science.[22] It is, rather, a philosophical thesis about the nature of reality. And as a philosophical thesis, materialism faces a number of difficult challenges.[23] Among other things, it has difficulty explaining the existence of rationality and cognition, goal-directed and law-like behavior in the universe, consciousness, and morality itself. Unfortunately, space considerations once again preclude a full-blown critique. Suffice it to say that materialism is a controversial thesis that is not entailed by any account of science.

Thus, human uniqueness is not at odds with science. It is, rather, at odds with a *materialistic interpretation* of the scientific data. The person who claims that evolutionary theory disproves human uniqueness is not making a scientific claim. He is making a philosophical claim about science that should be vigorously challenged.

So much for the Darwinian challenge.

There is, however, another challenge to human exceptionalism—one that is rooted in a particular set of moral and philosophical assumptions about the nature of value. This is the *speciesist* challenge. Singer and others following him argue that there is nothing special about being a member of the human species. Privileging humans over animals *simply* because they are human is morally arbitrary. It is wrong for the same reason that racism and sexism are wrong, for each focuses on qualities are that are deemed to be morally irrelevant. Even if humans have some feature that categorically distinguishes them from animals (e.g., rationality, an immaterial soul, language), Singer would object that these differences do not matter. Rather, what matters is simply the ability to feel pain. Anything capable of feeling pain counts as a member of the moral community. Since animals can obviously feel pain, animals count.

Other philosophers put forth different criteria. Philosopher Tom Regan, for example, argues that animals have rights because they are "subjects-of-a-life," which he cashes out in terms of a number of psychological properties.[24]

What these approaches have in common is the idea that moral status is something that extends beyond humans. For Singer, Regan, and others, the conditions for membership in the moral community are not customized for humans. Rather, they are broad enough to encompass a wide array of beings. Thus human exceptionalism amounts to an unjustified prejudice in favor of one's species.

Now, Singer and others have a point. It won't do to claim that human beings are superior to animals *just because* they are human. We need to flesh out just what exactly makes human beings special. If we can identify a morally significant feature that humans have but animals lack, then we have a foundation on which to justify human exceptionalism.

What would this feature be? Well, for the sake of presenting a complete argument in this chapter, I repeat here some of what is said in the previous chapter. In order to know who counts as a member of the moral community (and who does not), we need to know what *morality* itself is. We can't discern the criteria for membership in a group if we don't know anything about that group's nature or purpose. Nor can we discern who ought to enjoy the protections offered by morality without first knowing the point of morality. So, what is morality about?

The answer is simple and straightforward. All major moral theories agree that morality is fundamentally about the *pursuit of what is good and the avoidance of what is evil*. Whatever else we may say about its various nuances, this seems to be the core of what morality is. The whole point of morality, moral theorizing, and moral living is so that we may *be* moral—that is, to determine the truth about the good life so that it may be pursued through activity. Philosophers may disagree over *what* good and evil are, but *that* they are to be respectively pursued and avoided is something on which they can all agree.

Morality, then, is fundamentally about a certain type of *action*—namely, action in pursuit of what is good and action in avoidance of what is evil. Action of this kind, however, requires *knowledge* of what is good and what is evil, for one cannot act to pursue good and avoid evil if he does not know what good and evil are. Thus, the two fundamental objects of morality are knowledge and action.[25]

What does this tell us about the makeup of the moral community? Well, since morality is about action in pursuit of the good, it follows that membership in the moral community requires that a being be capable of (a) knowing what is good and evil and (b) acting for the sake of that knowledge. Whether the moral life consists of fulfilling duties, maximizing utility, or developing certain character dispositions, morality as such is something that can only be articulated, understood, and practiced by *rational beings.* Accordingly, a being has moral status only if it possesses a *rational nature.*[26] Now since all human beings have a rational nature, all human beings count as a member of the moral community.

Do animals have a rational nature? No, for at least two reasons.

First, if animals were able to reason in the sense relevant to moral status, then they would be under moral duties. The hawk would have a moral obligation not to eat a mouse, the lion would have a moral obligation not to eat a zebra, and wolves would have an obligation not to eat deer. All of this is simply absurd. Animals may be very intelligent, but they don't have the kind of intelligence necessary for moral agency.

Second, if some animals really are capable of rational agency, then they would have an intellect like ours. In that case, we should expect to see at least some semblance of civilization develop in the animal world. Yet we see none of this. The inability of animals to do anything like this is a sign that they aren't rational in the sense required for moral awareness. Sure, we might be able to train an orca to perform or teach a dog to do tricks, but to call this moral knowledge would be silly.

Singer, Regan, and others go wrong because they neglect to take into account the purpose of morality. The criteria they offer for moral significance have nothing to do with the pursuit of what is good and the avoidance of what is evil. Feeling pain sure *sounds* like a morally significant feature, but the mere ability to have perceptual experiences by itself has nothing to do with the purpose of morality. As humans, *our* pain experiences are morally significant, but only because they bear on the well-being of rational beings capable of moral agency. Outside of that context, pain experiences do not have any inherent moral significance. They just amount to a measure of well-being, which is something that plants and inanimate objects like computers also have. So the fact that animals are capable of feeling pain does not confer on them any kind of moral standing.

In sum, what makes us exceptional is the fact that we possess a rational nature. Possessing such a nature is a precondition for having moral worth of any kind. No other creature in the natural world can lay claim to this.

RESPONSIBLE DOMINION

Morality is about pursuing what is good and avoiding what is evil. For us, this means pursuing what is fulfilling of our humanity and avoiding what impedes it. Accordingly, we must eat, build shelters, and construct societies in order to reach our full potential. All of this requires the use of natural resources, whether it be meat and plants to nourish ourselves, wood to build shelters, or work animals and pets to provide help and companionship. Since all of these things are integral to our well-being, we have the *moral right* to use the resources we need to further our flourishing.

But even though we have dominion over nature, this dominion is not absolute. There are principles constraining the extent to which we may use plants, animals, and other natural resources for our own use. In the Judeo-Christian tradition, humans are called to be stewards over nature. This is because human authority is derived from God, who appoints humans as overseers over creation. Something similar to this view of stewardship can be supported by non-theological arguments.

It is obvious that our moral rights are limited. We can think of a moral right as a claim to some good or service necessary for our well-being. Rights exist in order to protect us as we do what morality requires. Thus, I have a right to life because I have the obligation to live well, and I cannot live well unless I am allowed access to goods required for me to flourish. Accordingly, I have rights to self-defense, education, and nutrition, for these all encompass goods that are integral to my flourishing. Now since rights exist to protect what is good for us, it follows that our rights are limited by the purpose for which they exist—namely, our well-being. Now since rights are supposed to protect our well-being, there is no such thing as a right to engage in activities that are destructive to our well-being. In fact, we have a *duty* to not engage in these sorts of activities.

Therefore, the right to use the environment for our purposes only extends so far. We do not have the right to use the environment in a way that significantly impairs human well-being. There is nothing *inherently* wrong with cutting down rainforests; draining swamps; genetically modifying plants, animals, and insects; or fracking for oil and gas; but these things can become wrong if done recklessly in a way that ends up harming humans. At the same time, responsibly engaging in these activities can and has resulted in much good and prosperity.[27] All this is an invitation to use caution and prudence in the way we interact with nature.

Of course, this is by no means easy. Not all practices are as clear-cut as one might hope them to be. Many have the dual effect of helping some while hurting others. Diverting water to power a hydroelectric dam may, we suppose, produce electricity that benefits large numbers of people. At the same time, the act of diverting water may negatively impact the agricultural prospects of farmers who suddenly find themselves deprived of an irrigation source or, conversely, find their lands flooded. Again, we must tread carefully. Human exceptionalism is not an excuse for us to be carefree and reckless.

PART IV
WHY SCRIPTURE MATTERS

7. The Old Testament's Case for Humanity Subduing and Ruling over Every Living Creature

WALTER C. KAISER JR.

THE VIEWS OF UTILITARIANISM AND CHRISTIAN ANIMAL RIGHTS

A question that is being asked more and more, especially by the younger generation, is "What is humanity's responsibility to the animal kingdom, in both its domestic and wildlife forms?" Surely the quick answer, from a biblical point of view, is not one of *utilitarianism*. A popular version of this view says we can do what we want with creatures in the animal kingdom, regardless of a creature's assumed pain or suffering caused either in raising these creatures or in the way they are slaughtered to be eaten.[1]

Another alternative is also inadequate. This is the view urged by the philosophy of the *Christian Animal Rights* (CAR). In their claim to be following the Bible, proponents of this view hold that animals, birds, and fish are creatures with intrinsic rights, which are the same—or even identical to—those bestowed on humans by their Creator. These rights guarantee life, liberty, and freedom to live their lives undisturbed by humans! Animals, which are also creatures of God, deserve the same level of respect we would show to humans since both are made by God.

The first view of pop-utilitarianism, it must be observed, assumes that humans are answerable only to themselves—as if God died and left all the creaturely order he made for humans to treat however they thought best to deal with them. However, God still claims, for instance, every beast of the field and all the cattle on the hills as his own possession (Psalm 50:10–12). Therefore, to abuse and exploit God's good creation would be to act in a way that is dishonoring to him. Moreover, contrary to the second view, just because humanity and animals have a common Creator, and both are formed "out of the ground" (as the CAR position assertively argues based on the flood narrative of Genesis 7), this is not an adequate basis for making humans and animals equal.

THE IMAGE OF GOD

Humans are uniquely made in the "image of God." They were commanded by God to "subdue" (Hebrew, *kabash*) and "rule over" (*radah*) the fish, the birds, and every living creature (Genesis 1:28). The more familiar King James Version translates *radah* as "have dominion over."

Now, some CAR advocates want to argue that Genesis 2:15 limits the scope of that human dominion over the other created beings exclusively to Adam and Eve's work in the garden of Eden. Moreover, they press the argument further: While humans are only ones made in the "image of God," this does not mean that animals are inferior beings to humans! In fact, a CAR person will argue that humans and animals partake of the same *nephesh chayah* (Genesis 1:30; 2:7), which is sometimes rendered in some contexts as "living soul" or "living being." However, that argument can be contested in this context, for what is shared by humans and animals is merely "the breath of life" (Genesis 6:17). But the fact that both share the "breath of life" does not mean that therefore both share the unique "image of God."

THE CASE FOR CHRISTIAN ANIMAL RIGHTS

The improbable CAR case can be described as follows: God originally planned the food chain for mortals to be exclusively one of vegetarianism their entire lives (pointing to Genesis 1:29 as evidence and misinterpreting Genesis 9:3). This would require humans to act not as "dominion-havers" but only as servant-caretakers over creation, without any dominion over birds, fish, or animals. There was to be no violence there, such as taking the life of animals, birds, or fish for nourishment, claims CAR. They were to eat only green plants and not meat of any type. That was God's original plan, or so it is claimed!

But with the fall of man and woman in the garden, humans and beasts no longer could or would live in harmony with each other, so God had to make a concession and give his permission for the human food chain to be changed. According to CAR theory, it must be stressed, this was a divine revision to God's original plan—one that now included fish, birds, and animals in the human diet.

The CAR group deliberately limits the scope of our human dominion, originally granted by God in Genesis 1:26–28, by arguing that the "image of God" did not entail any real or actual ("ontological") inferiority of the animals to mortals, for it referred merely to humankind's sense of morality—one in which humans should mirror God's holiness and justice. The CAR activists believe such a non-ontological argument for animals is justified by the following:

(1) animals and humans have a common Creator;
(2) animals have a right to their own place in the world; the world does not belong solely to humans;
(3) animals and humans were both created on the same day;
(4) God's original plan for humans was for them to have servant-based work and non-violent work; and
(5) since God takes the initiative to rest on the seventh day, resting and tranquility on the seventh day are the goal of the entire created order.

To all of the CAR arguments, however, the following must be said:

(1) God mandated Adam to name the animals, which suggests some type of authoritarian position over them;
(2) the Creation Mandate to the first couple was for them to "subdue" or "have authority over" the created order;
(3) according to other Scriptures, God put in place an animal food chain from the very beginning, indicating that predatory activity is not a result of the fall (Job 38:39–40; 39:26–30; 41:1, 14; Psalm 104:21–29); this food chain is even called "good" (Psalm 104:28)!

Unfortunately, CAR activists have *re*-translated the two commands in this mandate to read instead to "have mastery" and "to settle" the animals. But the Hebrew will not allow that reading.

CAR understands that the "image of God" (Genesis 1:26) does not mean animals were created inferior to humans. Rather, they say, the fall introduced the violence against animals that came later, with the sin of the couple in the garden and Noah's flood. But this point, sadly, fails to note that the "image of God" included

(1) the human ability to speak/talk (which no animal possesses);
(2) our ability to love (which is not enjoyed in animals to the same extent as in humans);
(3) our treasure of residual knowledge, which has not been shown to exist in animals (Colossians 3:10); and

(4) our being called in "righteousness and holiness"—a spiritual capacity that is exclusive to humans (Ephesians 4:24).

Humanity is much different from the rest of the created order!

In addition, CAR inexplicably denies that the formation of man and woman was actually the real goal of creation. But that is not the way Genesis reads, for when God created man and woman, he did not just call his work this time "good," as he had done so frequently up to the point in the creation narrative before humans were created; instead, when he finished making Adam and Eve, God called that work "very good."

THE SACRIFICE OF ANIMALS IN THE OLD TESTAMENT

Of course, the sacrificial system of the Old Testament presents an enormous challenge to CAR activists' view against killing any animals used for sacrifices in the worship of the Lord in the Old Testament. How, CAR advocates often complain, could God love birds and other animals and yet require their deaths as sacrifices to him? Therefore, these activists must begin their argument by denying that God even ordered such an act in connection with the atonement for sin. For confirmation of their denial of this divine requirement of sacrifice, which goes directly in the face of what Scripture teaches, they attempt to demonstrate that the prophets likewise showed that God was not asking so much for animals to be killed for sacrifice as he was looking for something else.

They argue this case by giving an outright misinterpretation of the following texts, given here as a sample:

- "The multitude of your sacrifices—what are they to me?" says the LORD. "I have more than enough of burnt offerings, of rams and the fat of fattened animals ... Stop bringing meaningless offerings! Your incense is detestable to me ... Learn to do right; seek justice. Defend the oppressed. Take up the cause of the fatherless; plead the case of the widow" (Isaiah 1:11–17, NIV);
- "'This is what the LORD Almighty, the God of Israel, says: Go ahead, add your burnt offerings to your other sacrifices and eat the meat yourselves! For when I brought your ancestors out of Egypt and spoke to them, I did not just give them commands about burnt offerings and sacrifices, but I gave them this command: Obey me and I will be your God and you will be my people'" (Jeremiah 7:21–23, NIV);

- "I hate, I despise your religious festivals; your assemblies are a stench to me … Though you bring choice fellowship offerings, I will have no regard for them" (Amos 5:21–22, NIV);
- "With what shall I come before the LORD and bow down before the exalted God? Shall I come before him with burnt offerings, with calves … He has shown all you, O mortal, what is good. And what does the LORD require of you? To act justly and to love mercy and to walk humbly with your God" (Micah 6:6–8, NIV).

But as any serious reader of the Bible knows, these prophets were not condemning the use of sacrifices, or the killing of animals per se, but they were challenging the people's rote presentation of these sacrifices merely in an outward, external, or ritualistic way. Doing so, they assumed, meant that the simple act of sacrificing was good enough in itself without any accounting for where their heart was in the whole act of sacrificing! God had indeed commanded that sacrifices should be offered, but not as a formal routine act that did not demand the wholehearted commitment of the will and sincere attitude of the inner heart from the one offering the sacrifice.

King David came to this very realization the hard way. After he committed adultery with Bathsheba, he learned that during those nine months of her pregnancy, when he had apparently decided to just stonewall God and not admit to him the whole incident, he was unable to soothe his conscience merely by presenting one sacrifice after another. It all amounted to just so much bull! In fact, this went on for so long a time that David felt as if all his bones were going to snap from being so spiritually dried up and destitute of real inner health. God was, for the moment, not so much interested in the mere routine of sacrifices and offerings per se as he was in the priority of a broken and contrite heart: "You do not delight in sacrifice, or I would bring it; you do not take pleasure in burnt offerings. My sacrifice, O God, is a broken spirit; a broken and contrite heart you, God, will not despise" (Psalm 51:16–17, NIV).

Now, to bolster the case CAR makes for why it is that humans and animals no longer live in harmony, these activists[2] propose a link between the fall of humanity in the garden of Eden and the happenings in the life of Noah. Three points are used by the CAR advocates to show this connection:

(1) the fall of humanity in the garden of Eden broke the harmony between humankind and the whole order of creation;

(2) violence came into the created order because of the sin and fall of humans and the collapse of society in Noah's day so that God had to send the flood on the earth; and

(3) the fall led to despair, so that creation currently groans in travail waiting for God's redemption (Romans 8:20–22).

A major part of the violence, it is further argued, that was introduced into creation as a result of the fall involved eating meat—misinterpreting Genesis 6:11–12. Thus, the animals were corrupted to the point where they became carnivores—once again misusing Genesis 6:12–17!

GOD GIVES PERMISSION FOR MORTALS TO EAT MEAT

But surely CAR advocates understand from reading the Scriptures that God gave his permission to eat meat in Genesis 9:3–4; he only withheld eating blood along with the meat. The CAR interpreters, however, do not believe God granted this permission happily; it was merely a concession and a permission to accommodate humanity's violent nature. Some in this group claim that the ban on eating blood was God's way of saying that killing animals was shameful and an act he disapproved of.[3]

However, this ban *instead* signified that God owned all life, since life was in the blood (Leviticus 17:14). *That* was the key reason why blood was to be excluded from this permission: the life was owned exclusively by God.

DID GOD AUTHORIZE ABUSE OF ANIMALS?

But there is one final point we must raise. Does our argument for humanity's dominion over the animals also show that animals can be exploited at will by humans? In other words, has humanity been given carte blanche permission to impose on creation whatever it wishes? It was not too long ago that Lynn White Jr. gave his stinging indictment, especially zeroing in on Bible-believers who took the words "subdue" and "have dominion," as he puts it, for their autocratic and dominant abuse of the environment and nature.[4]

White, however, was at fault for laying the blame of the ecological intolerance of modernity on Scripture, for the blame really rested on poor interpreters of Scripture. But the drive to assert full equality of all of God's creatures on a somewhat misunderstood pattern of St. Francis of Assisi is likewise to be avoided. To be without a realization that God created men and women to be formed in his own image and that they were given the task of responsibly ruling and having dominion over the created forms and were answerable directly to God for that conduct is to adopt an inverted view of world and to demean the created order as God set it up. Of course, animals, birds, and fish are just as much creatures of God, but they were not meant in God's plan to be equal with humanity or to have a like mission of ruling and having dominion over all the rest of creation as God declared it was so for men and women.

CONCLUSION

The CAR position has not demonstrated that the Old Testament denies or even condemns men and women for using animals for their food. To achieve such a reading from the Old Testament, one must cherry-pick certain phrases and verses out of their biblical context and then give them a spin not consistent with the author's intentions.

Despite their misguided treatment of the Old Testament, CAR advocates have nevertheless gotten this right: their emphasis urges farmers, hunters, and just plain ordinary stewards of all God's created beings to handle these creatures in life and also to prepare them for the food chain in a way that is respectful and pleasing to God. God's creatures are not junk: they were made by him and were to be cared for by those he gave the added blessing of being made in his image as they subdued and exercised dominion over them.

8. Veggie Tales?
PETA, Paganism,
and Other Vegan Confusions
PAUL COPAN

In the previous chapter, we read about the Old Testament evidence that in no way undermines meat-eating but rather permits and supports it. This chapter and the next build on this foundation. First we consider further misrepresentations of the Jewish-Christian Scriptures, then we note the pagan origins of mandatory veganism, and finally we expand on the Old Testament's perspective on meat-eating. Since the Old Testament serves as the backdrop to the New Testament's permission to eat meat, in the next chapter we explore the New Testament witness in detail.

THREE VEXING VEGGIE TALES
During the mid-1990s, Phil Vischer dreamed up *Veggie Tales*—a series of children's videos starring Bob the Tomato and Larry the Cucumber. These animated vegetables presented lessons to children about virtue and faith, largely drawing on Jesus's teaching and the lives of biblical characters. This idea-turned-sensation would end up selling 65 million videos as well as entertaining—and hopefully instructing—many youngsters.

A few years later, a different kind of Veggie Tale emerged. In 1999, the organization PETA sponsored a billboard campaign that inserted Jesus into its agenda. They claimed that "Jesus was a vegetarian." The idea they were trying to sell was this: If you claim to follow Jesus, you should be a vegetarian too.[1] Now, the fact that this billboard comes from PETA should prompt us to be suspicious. After all, PETA's founder, Ingrid Newkirk, herself claimed, "A rat is a pig is a boy is a dog." This is a profoundly *anti*-Christian pronouncement, repudiating the biblical assumption that humans are distinct from and elevated above the animals. Humans are made in the image of God and are called not only to love and worship God but to be co-rulers and co-stewards with God over creation (Genesis 1:26–28).

Now, the billboard's message is one that a growing number of Christians in the academy and beyond have embraced as the truly consistent biblical view. It is called "prescriptive Christian vegetarianism." Let's briefly unpack that: *Christians* allegedly have a *duty* ("prescriptive") to *avoid eating meat* of any kind in favor of a plant-based diet ("vegetarianism").

Now just a quick definitional matter here: *vegetarianism* typically represents a plant-based diet (which may include fish, eggs, or dairy, but no animal flesh); *veganism* takes a moral position, opposing not only eggs, fish, and dairy but also the manufacture of products made with leather, silk, fur, and wool—or animals used in circuses, for example. For our purposes, we'll use the term *vegetarianism* in a more restricted *moral* sense that considers the consumption of animals to be unethical or, at best, to be avoided. There are some Christians who acknowledge meat-eating is permitted by Scripture, but others treat meat-eating as inherently immoral or unspiritual—a position that is itself denounced by Scripture as a false teaching. But the more lenient position is also problematic, as we'll observe.

Here's another similarly troubling Veggie Tale. Charles Camosy, professor of Christian ethics at Fordham University, claims that it is inherently wrong to eat the flesh of non-human animals. Why? These animals are created to be the *companions*—not the *food*—of human beings.[2] In order to maintain this position, Camosy must downgrade biblical authority. He insists, "Not everything that Paul says in his letters is inspired by God."[3] And he adds that the "pro-life" position—regarding unborn humans as intrinsically valuable beings—must extend beyond humans to include animals as well.

Consider a third disturbing Veggie Tale. Philosophy professor Daniel Dombrowski is on the advisory board of the Christian Vegetarian Association—a group of Christians who endeavor to "respectfully encourage healthy, God-honoring plant-based nutrition." Of course, the clear implication of this assertion is that meat-eating *dishonors* God. Now, Dombrowski rightly notes the fact that the divine image in humans doesn't give them license to treat animals any way they want.[4] But Dombrowski is wrong to claim that the ancient Hebrews' view of humans as "the crown of creation" is actually "a status which denigrates animals."[5] The fact that humans are made "a little lower than God" (Psalm 8:5) isn't a denigration of humans. And the fact that animals are made lower than humans is simply highlighting our human distinctiveness as God's image-bearers. After all, humans were made with a distinct range of capacities—spiritual, moral, volitional, relational, and rational; these are qualities that enable them to relate to God and act as moral agents—characteristics animals do not have.

The tale gets worse, though. Dombrowski even *denounces* Jesus—yes, Jesus—as complicit in the mistreatment of animals. Reflecting on the portrayal of the Gadarene demoniac in Mark 5 and its Gospel parallels, he states that Jesus "showed indifference (if not cruelty) to nonhumans when he unnecessarily forced 2,000 swine to hurl themselves into the sea."[6] Actually, this "swine dive" was a *demon*-induced act. Furthermore, Jesus's greater concern for just *one* demonized man over against a large herd of swine should tell us something: this one man had far greater value in the eyes of Jesus than many swine. What mattered far more was this man's spiritual, psychological, and even physical restoration and liberation. If we have to choose between Jesus and Dombrowski to get an accurate perspective on humans and animals, the authoritative Son of God is the obvious choice.

My recommendation for Camosy and Dombrowski is to just come clean and drop the "Christian" from their label; they should simply call themselves "prescriptive vegetarians." After all, why appeal to the Christian faith or dogma when the authority of Moses, Jesus, and Paul are called into question? Such moves are a perversion of the Christian tradition. Not surprisingly, Dombrowski's book—which connects vegetarianism to the ancient Greeks and the Romans—is endorsed by "animalist" philosopher Peter Singer.

Various other Christian scholars have attempted to "enlarge our moral universe" to make room for animals as part of an ethic of compassion towards all of God's creatures.[7] One "Christian universalist" writer, Hannah Hurnard (1905-1990), exhibited a similar misguided compassion in which she viewed "the beasts and the birds" as our "little brothers and sisters." She believed that harm to any animals was harm to the Body of Christ.[8]

For various reasons, the claims of these thinkers are flawed. Their over-exalted picture of animals—again, flowing from a misguided compassion—doesn't faithfully express Christian theology. These thinkers should take better care not to allow their tale to wag the dogma of the Christian faith.

PRESCRIPTIVE PAGAN VEGETARIANISM VS. THE BIBLICAL FAITH

Various pagan religions—much like modern animal rights activists—have taken an elevated view of animals, which often results in diminishing humanity. The biblical faith presents quite a contrast to this. As God's image-bearers, we humans are called to be *stewards* or *caretakers with*

God over creation (Genesis 1:26–28). Our unique status doesn't entail permission to abuse animals. Proper care for animals is part of our stewardship (Deuteronomy 22:1–4, 6, 10; 25:4; Proverbs 12:10; Jonah 4:11). But care for animals doesn't entail that animals have "rights" or that they are moral beings.[9] If this were the case, should we not stop lions and cheetahs from attacking gazelles and zebras, whose alleged "rights" are being violated? Why not regard predators as serial killers? As noted in chapter 5, whatever interesting and remarkable qualities certain animals have, they still do not have what it takes to be part of a moral—or spiritual—community. They simply do not have what it takes to bear that burden.[10] (In 1996, Wes Jamison—this book's coeditor—conducted a large-scale survey of animal rights and welfare activists. Over 90 percent believed animals have reasoning abilities along with moral capacities to make moral choices. However, they did not think that animals could make immoral or evil choices!)

Some prescriptive Christian vegetarians shift focus from the Scriptures and argue that we should be *more principled* omnivores. *If* we are going to eat meat as God's people, we should at least opt to eat, say, chickens and eggs from farms that utilize "compassionate" practices. We should avoid meat products from intensive animal farming ("factory farming") or large-scale fishing. Of course, any principled meat-eater would agree that we should take care to avoid overfishing and depleting resources.[11] That said, humans are finding more and more efficient ways of providing abundant tasty, nutritious meat products for multitudes—especially in the hog farming industry (see chapter 10). Despite complaints about intensive animal farming, the more fundamental question is whether or not animals are moral beings and thus have rights. In chapters 4 and 5, we saw that this a problematic assumption, but we can spell out a further reason to challenge the idea of "animal rights."

Consider: if nature is all the reality there is ("naturalism"), and everything is the product of mindless, valueless material processes, why think that *anything* of value—whether humans *or* animals—should emerge from all of this? But if a good God exists and that God desires to relate to human beings, then the appearance of valuable rights-bearing humans is unsurprising. But why expect value and dignity to arise from the slime of valuelessness? If atheists hold to animal rights, they will be borrowing objective moral value from a view like the biblical faith—a view that happens to support human rights but not animal rights. It is this supremely valuable God who is the basis for intrinsically valuable rights-bearing human beings.

And when the naturalist/atheist considers "animal abuse" to be "evil" or "wrong," where does such a standard come from in a Godless universe? After all, evil is a departure from the way things ought to be. But this presupposes a design plan, from which evil is a deviation. If nature simply *is*, why think anything *ought* to be a certain way? To call something evil presupposes a standard of goodness or design. The atheist or naturalist then has *two* problems to deal with: the problem of evil and the problem of goodness. These make no sense if nature is all the reality there is.

Apart from these philosophical problems, we can say that, in principle, *absolute prescriptive vegetarianism (meat-eating as inherently unspiritual) is not Christian,* and *it is not even remotely supported by Scripture.* Indeed, it is *anti*-Christian—teachings that stem from anti-gospel "elementary principles of this world" (Colossians 2:16–23) and "doctrines of demons" (1 Timothy 4:1–5).

Yet some continue to push an essentially pagan perspective onto the Scriptures to make them say what they do not endorse. Here is another text commonly appealed to: the example of Daniel and his three friends in Babylon in Daniel 1. This passage indicates that these Jewish young men avoided eating meat from the king's table; they requested eating only vegetables and drinking only water for a fixed period of time ("ten days"), and in the end they turned out be healthier than those who ate from the king's table.

Now, was their superior physical health *due to* their vegetarianism?[12] Is some *norm* being prescribed here? No—on both questions. This passage tells us that Daniel "would not defile himself with the king's choice food or with the wine which he drank" (Daniel 1:8). The reason for this vegetarian diet is that Daniel and his friends would otherwise be compromising their Jewish faith—perhaps because these foods were contaminated by idolatrous worship or possibly the foods were not kosher (see Leviticus 11; Deuteronomy 14). Some kind of *defilement* was to be avoided.

So Daniel wasn't a prescriptive Jewish vegetarian, and this becomes more obvious later in the book. There we're told that a mourning Daniel was fasting from eating meat and drinking wine—but *only* for three weeks: "I did not eat any tasty food, nor did meat or wine enter my mouth, nor did I use any ointment at all *until the entire three weeks were completed*" (Daniel 10:3, italics mine). Clearly, eating meat (not simply vegetables) and drinking wine (not just water) were simply part of Daniel's ordinary diet.

Although prescriptive vegetarianism condemns all meat-eating as immoral, this stands in stark opposition to Scripture. As we've seen, *meat-eating abolitionists often reject the God-ordained distinction between humans and animals.* Secondly, *prescriptive vegetarianism is actually rooted in paganism and various Eastern religions.* How so? It is typically associated with reincarnation, which suggests a continuity between humans and animals. In this case, one's soul in a *human* body could appear in an *animal* body in the next life. So then, don't even eat animals! As Christian philosopher James Reichmann points out, "Historically there has been a distinct link between the theory of the transmigration of souls and the practice of vegetarianism as a moral imperative."[13] This idea of reincarnation stands against the tide of biblical doctrine: "people are destined to die once, and after that to face judgment" (Hebrews 9:27).

Thirdly, *the Bible gives robust justification for meat-eating; in itself, eating meat is permitted and even celebrated as a gift from God.* In the rest of this chapter, we note the Old Testament's positive view of eating meat. In the next chapter, the example of Jesus and the teachings of the apostle Paul and the rest of the New Testament pronounce a blessing on meat-eating as a gift from God. Meat-eating isn't mandatory, but it is certainly permitted. What's more, as we'll see, Jesus not only opens the door *more* widely for meat-eating than does the Old Testament; Paul even *condemns* those who prohibit meat-eating for spiritual reasons: doing so undermines the spirit of the gospel message itself (Romans 14:2).

Before we look specifically at the incarnate Christ's and other New Testament authorities' views on meat-eating, we should take a glance backward at carnivorosity in the Old Testament. This better informs us as we look at the New Testament in the next chapter.

THE OLD TESTAMENT TRADITION OF MEAT-EATING

As opposed to the previous Veggie Tales, the doctrine of creation includes two important themes that actually counter prescriptive Christian vegetarianism: (a) the goodness of meat-eating as a gift from God, as well as (b) a food chain God put into place from the very outset of his good creation. Let's look at these briefly.

First, *eating meat is a blessing from God.* Consider Deuteronomy 14:26, which reads, "You may spend the money for whatever your heart desires: for oxen, or sheep, or wine, or strong drink, or whatever your heart desires; and there you shall eat in the presence of the LORD your God and rejoice, you and your household."

Just two chapters earlier, God permits the Israelites to "slaughter and eat meat within any of your gates, whatever you desire, according to the blessing of the LORD your God which He has given you; the unclean and the clean may eat of it, as of the gazelle and the deer" (Deuteronomy 12:15). A few verses later, the same theme of eating meat according to one's desire is repeated: "you may eat meat, whatever you desire" (v. 20).

We could add any number of passages that support meat-eating. Consider the sacrificial system that makes provision for priests to eat meat from the offerings (for example, Leviticus 6:29; 7:6). Or note how God himself sustains his prophet Elijah with meat. In 1 Kings 17, ravens bring the prophet Elijah "bread and meat" while he is in hiding from King Ahab (v. 6). This operation is due to the direction of God: "I have commanded the ravens to provide for you there" (v. 4). In these scenarios, meat-eating is a blessing from God.

Not only is meat-eating a blessing in the *first* creation; it is also a blessing in the *second* creation—the new heavens and new earth. The Old Testament prophets looked forward to a final day of feasting with meat in the new heavens and earth: "a lavish banquet … a banquet of aged wine, choice pieces with marrow" (Isaiah 25:6–8). This meat-eating is to take place in that permanent future "Golden Age" in which there will be no harm or danger.

What then is the point about carnivores eating straw or the lion being together with the lamb—as well as other pairings of wild and domesticated animals (Isaiah 11, 35, 65, and 66)? We have reasons to think that this language about the new creation shouldn't be taken literally. After all, we read that a person who *dies* at the age of one hundred will be "accursed" and considered a mere youth (Isaiah 65:20)—and *this* is in the new heavens and earth! Of course, this is a metaphorical way of referring to longevity—something like "We're going to live an incredibly long time during this final age." Similarly, rather than speaking of permanent vegetarianism, such texts are merely referring to danger removal or the domestication of all possible danger. And so a nursing child can play by a cobra's nest without fear (Isaiah 11:8). In other words, we should be careful about pressing the lion-and-lamb imagery too far. After all, Isaiah 35:9 states, "no lion will be there" in the final creation! That is, there will be "no evil or harm" in all God's holy mountain (Isaiah 65:25).

Second, *God put an animal food chain in place from the very beginning.* Prescriptive Christian vegetarians will often appeal to a world prior to the fall as being a place of vegetarianism for all of God's creatures. One publication of the Christian Vegetarian Association—*Joyful, Compassionate Eating*—makes a number of misleading Scripture claims and some outright falsehoods. One false claim is that animals were made to be "helpers" for the man in Eden (no, it was the *woman* who was to be a "help [*ezer*]" to the man—just like God is Israel's "help" [Psalm 121:2]). Here's another problematic claim: a plant-based diet is the ideal diet—one that glorifies God—based on the assumed vegetarianism set forth at the end of Genesis 1.[14] Is this true?

Now, although some Christian readers may disagree with my response, I believe that a very plausible theological case can be made to challenge this ideal-Eden-diet claim. This is one of several different

Christian positions one can take in response to prescriptive Christian vegetarianism.

For one thing, the fossil record clearly indicates that before humans were on the scene, predatory activity and animal death were abundantly evident.[15] *Animal* death took place before humans fell away from God (Genesis 3). Now, some Christians (not necessarily prescriptive vegetarians) argue that animal death came through Adam's sin (based on Romans 5), but this is incorrect. Rather, *human* death is in view. Adam's "transgression" brought "condemnation," but the second Adam, Jesus, brought "justification" for all people (Romans 5:18). This doesn't relate to the animal kingdom.

Genesis 1 is making a literary and theological point. It emphasizes harmony and God's provision of edible plants for humans and animals alike (Genesis 1:29–30). Indeed, ultimately *all* creaturely diets depend in some way on plants; so whether directly or indirectly, all creatures—including carnivores—benefit from plant-eating. Now the harmony presented in Genesis 1 generally *avoids* talking about nature's bloodiness. But even so, what else, say, could it mean to have dominion or "rule over the fish of the sea" (Genesis 1:26) except to *eat* them?

Beyond this, *other* Old Testament passages make clear that God's original creation involves predatory activity. For example, Psalm 104—a *creation* psalm—indicates that God graciously provides prey for the lion (v. 21). And God the Creator takes away the breath of animals, and they die and return to the dust (v. 29). Yet all of his creatures have food, and they are "satisfied with good" (v. 28). Notice that this is the same word *good* (*tob* in the Hebrew) that is used in Genesis 1. The food chain *isn't* viewed as an evil, according to Scripture.

The book of Job reinforces this "creational food chain" theme. We are probably familiar with God's climactic response to Job's demanding spirit. Job repeatedly calls for an audience with God (e.g., Job 23), and so God shows up and asks where Job was at the creation. And what kinds of things did God create? Dangerous carnivorous animals! This includes the hawk, which brings bloody morsels to its nestlings, which "suck up blood" (Job 39:26–30). God also mentions the "fierce" Leviathan (crocodile) with "fearsome teeth" (41:1, 14). God refers to "prey for the lion" and lions that "crouch in their dens" and "lie in wait in their lair" (38:39–40). God even "prepares for the raven its nourishment" (39:41): ravens are omnivores, and they eat mostly meat.

Old Testament scholar John Goldingay comments,

> Genesis's readers know that the animal world does not live in harmony but lives on the basis of dog eat dog. Genesis 1 implies that this is not

God's intention, but neither is it simply the result of a human "Fall." Animal inclination to kill and eat other animals is built into their nature as animals and is part of the "goodness" of creation, yet holding them back from doing that [i.e., for humans] is part of humanity's vocation.[16]

So, the *goodness* of creation doesn't imply its *perfection* or *completion* (Romans 8:19–23). Humans still have the task to "tame" or "keep back" (*kabash*) the forces of nature (see Genesis 1:28).[17] As we've seen, to "rule" over certain animals suggests the possibility of "eating." This all fits what 1 Timothy 4:3–4 indicates: *humans are permitted to eat anything of God's good creation*, and we must do so with thankful hearts.

9. What Would Jesus Eat?
From Kosher to Everything
PAUL COPAN

We're perhaps familiar with "WWJD" printed on T-shirts, bracelets, or wall plaques: "What would Jesus do?" For our purposes, we are looking at *WWJE*: "What would Jesus eat?"—or more precisely, what foods did Jesus *actually* eat, and which foods would he *permit* (and even *commend*) his followers and humanity to eat? The short answer includes all manner of meats, and not simply kosher ones. As we've seen, various prescriptive Christian vegetarians pick and choose verses here and there in desperate attempts to support their views (e.g., Daniel and his friends eating just vegetables in Babylon). We should look at the sweep of Scripture and should take seriously the example and teaching of our Savior and supreme authority, Jesus of Nazareth, and the apostolic witness after Jesus.

KNOWLEDGE AND THE CHRISTIAN FAITH AS PUBLIC TRUTH
Faith and Reason
We soon look at Jesus's views about diet and discipleship, and some readers may wish to jump ahead to the next section to do so. But we should perhaps address one question that may lurk in the mind of the Bible-believing reader: "Although *I* believe in the Bible and take its authority seriously about permission to eat meat and about all other aspects of life, how do I communicate this to people who *don't* share my confidence in biblical authority?" Now, we could utilize philosophical arguments to lay out our case, as presented in chapters 5 and 6. This is an example of appropriating God's "natural revelation": God reveals something of his existence and character through reason, creation, conscience, and human

experience (e.g., Isaiah 28:23–29), and we can, by God's grace, seek to persuade others by using these means.

Even so, the question before us ultimately comes down to *knowledge*: Can we *know* that God's special revelation in Jesus Christ is true and thus speak with confidence to outsiders to the faith? Our culture recognizes that having knowledge—not merely opinions—qualifies one to speak with authority. Assuming that we are properly interpreting Scripture, we have a knowledge-source to which we can appeal.

But isn't the appeal to Scripture a matter of "faith"? A lot of people misunderstand the term *faith* in the biblical tradition. For some religions, it may be a blind leap—one taken without regard to evidence and that refuses to consider anything that could potentially falsify it. Mark Twain described faith as "believing what you know ain't so." Contrary to this and other such caricatures, faith in the biblical tradition is a *personal commitment* and *trust* in light of what we take to be true. It isn't a "blind leap." In fact, faith (personal trust) is perfectly compatible with reason and evidence.

The late philosopher Mortimer Adler nicely illustrated the point. He came to realize that he had all the evidence he needed to see that the Christian faith was fully intellectually sound and most reasonable. But this wasn't enough. This kind of intellectualized "faith" is like that of the demons' knowledge, who also believe there is one God (James 2:19). Yet Adler never really trusted in Christ personally ("faith"). He experienced a late-life conversion on a hospital bed, confessing that even philosophical reasoning in itself could not bring him into relationship with God: "I simply did not wish to exercise a will to believe." Again, faith is a *volitional* stance. He wrote,

> The soundest rational argument for God's existence could only carry us to the edge of the chasm that separated the philosophical affirmation of God's existence from the religious belief in God. What is usually called "a leap of faith" is needed to carry anyone across the chasm. But the leap of faith is usually misunderstood as being a progress from having insufficient reasons for affirming God's existence to a state of greater certitude in that affirmation. That is not the case. The leap of faith consists in going from the conclusion of a merely philosophical theology to a religious belief in a God that has revealed himself as a loving, just and merciful Creator of the cosmos, a God to be loved, worshiped and prayed to.[1]

Adler came to embrace God as *his* Father and Jesus as *his* Lord. By the work of the Spirit, he personalized the evidence. God can and does use reason and evidence to bring people to faith—just as he uses illness, crisis, death, guilt, and disappointment to do so.

In Scripture, public signs and wonders often inspire faith—like the miracles in John's Gospel (John 20:30–31; 10:25, 38). Paul, who once persecuted the church before the risen Jesus appeared to him, furnished his readers with a list of eyewitnesses to the resurrected Jesus (1 Corinthians 15:3–8)—a list that was passed on from the very start of the Jerusalem church. The earliest Christians attested to events that were not "done in a corner" (Acts 26:26) and that the apostles were eyewitnesses of Jesus's ministry, death, and resurrection (Luke 1:2; 2 Peter 1:16). They proclaimed the stuff of history—the kind that is available for public scrutiny. The biblical faith is historical, rational, and well-grounded, and it takes its stand as *public truth*—as a knowledge tradition. Thus, Jesus—when he speaks on meat-eating or anything else—speaks with authority as the full revelation of God (John 14:9), and we have many good reasons to take that authority as trustworthy.

Taking Confidence in the Christian Knowledge Tradition
While we can't go into much detail here, I have written elsewhere on the compatibility of faith and reason.[2] Resources abound regarding the Bible's textual and historical reliability,[3] the credibility and even documentation of miracles,[4] the harmony of the Christian faith and science,[5] and the historicity of Jesus's bodily resurrection.[6] While Christians can affirm important truths and ideals and other glimmers of light in other traditional religions and cultures, the person of Jesus stands out as savingly unique. He is the embodiment of the world's greatest ideals, philosophies, epic stories, moral truths, and traditions. He is, as C. S. Lewis said, "myth became fact."

Indeed, the biblical faith stands out in the following ways from the world's philosophies and religions:

- *Jesus's claims and actions* went far beyond that of other world religious leaders. He claims to forgive sin, to be the Lord of the Sabbath/creation and the final Judge. He is correctly charged (by his enemies) of claiming to stand in the place of God (John 5:18).
- *The earliest Christians bore witness to an exalted Jesus who shared in the divine identity*—even though they were fiercely monotheistic Jews who strongly opposed idolatry.
- In the Christian faith, *God the Creator sacrifices himself for his broken creatures, who are "enemies"* (Romans 5:6–10). King Jesus has scars to show this (John 20:20; also Revelation 5:6).

- *Many world religions and philosophies want to claim Jesus for themselves as an authority.* Jesus is held in the highest esteem across the religious spectrum, which further indicates his rather unique standing.
- *The Christian faith is publicly checkable* (Luke 1:1–4; 1 Corinthians 15:3–8; 2 Peter 1:16–18)—unlike other world religions.
- *The Christian faith uniquely proclaims salvation by God's gracious gift*; it doesn't rest on human self-achievement or merit.
- *Jesus rose bodily from the dead in confirmation of his claims* (1 Corinthians 15)—unlike other religious leaders.

In addition to these unique features, we can add that the biblical understanding of reality—its "metaphysic" or worldview—can readily account for a host of features in the universe that a naturalistic, materialistic world cannot. To appeal to science in order to make sense of these features is misguided. For one thing, to study the physical world, non-physical minds must exist. Also, before science is even possible, the world of nature must first exist. The universe has not always existed but rather came into existence a finite time ago; something independent of the physical universe—something like a powerful Creator—would make sense of this. A Big Bang needs a Big Banger!

Also, the mathematically rich fundamental laws of nature and the fine-tuning of the rational universe are well accounted for by a remarkable Mind or Intelligence. In addition, a supremely self-aware being would make excellent sense of the existence of consciousness—unlike non-conscious matter somehow producing consciousness. And the existence of a supremely valuable being makes excellent sense of human uniqueness and value, including intrinsic human dignity, human rights, and moral duties; here too it's difficult to see how valueless matter could somehow produce morally valuable beings. Furthermore, the vast array of the world's beauty—from sunsets to the lilies of the field to the Northern Lights—makes sense if there is an ingenious creative being behind it all.

These features of the universe are highly probable if God exists and wants to relate to human beings; these features aren't surprising or unnatural at all. They are nicely explained by a powerful, good, intelligent, self-aware, rational being. However, to say that these features of the universe somehow emerged from mindless, non-conscious, valueless, non-rational, material deterministic processes is to hang on to a remote improbability upon improbability. We have no reason to expect the kind of outcome we have. Here is an important point: *Even those "secularists" who claim that animals have value and rights are still left with the difficulty of how anything of value could emerge from valueless processes.* What's worse is that animal liberationists who denounce causing "sentient" beings any pain are strangely silent on the abortion issue—namely, when it comes to causing pain to "sentient" human beings in the womb. The "silent scream" of the unborn is generally ignored by these advocates of "compassion."

Suffice it to say that we can speak with confident knowledge about God's existence and about God's revelation in Jesus Christ in history and the Scriptures. In addition to God's revelation in creation, conscience, reason, and human experience, biblical faith and tradition can bring illumination where alternative worldviews simply make assertions without justification—like "animals have rights."

As we noted previously, arguments in defense of the Christian faith are useless apart from the workings of God's Spirit. God can use solid reasons to help unbelievers (and believers too!) to overcome honest doubts and to assist them in becoming (or being more faithful) disciples of Jesus. Sheer reasoning—or suffering or financial crises or the burden of guilt—won't by itself lead people to trust in God (faith). God's empowering Spirit is needed.

With this important qualification in place, let's shift from some of these questions about justification and knowledge to the topic of Jesus and his apostles as authoritative voices on the matter of meat-eating.

JESUS'S OWN ACTIONS SUPPORT THE LEGITIMACY OF MEAT-EATING
Jesus Commanded Appropriating the Old Testament Sacrificial System During His Ministry

During Jesus's earthly ministry, he emphasized the spirit of "compassion" over external "sacrifice" (Matthew 9:13; 12:7). He nevertheless urged people to follow Old Testament sacrificial procedures when circumstances required them. For example, he told a leper he had healed, "go, show yourself to the priest and present the offering that Moses commanded, as a testimony to them" (Matthew 8:4). This cleansed leper was to follow the protocols of Leviticus 14. But what did this procedure include? The sacrificial deaths of a bird and two lambs (vv. 1–20). Jesus did not prohibit—but indeed stood behind—the authoritative sacrificial system instituted for national Israel under Moses. He was born "under the Law" of Moses (Galatians 4:4–5), and he lived out its precepts as a faithful Israelite. This sacrificial legislation remained in place for God's people until the once-for-all atoning death of Jesus on the cross (Hebrews 9:11–14). Though this is not a case of eating meat, *Jesus's command here involves animal death, which he does not view as inherently immoral.*

Jesus Permitted and Encouraged Meat-Eating in Various Ways

The Son of God permitted and even encouraged the eating of meat in the following ways. First, *Jesus regularly attended feasts that involved the eating of meat.* For example, Jesus celebrated the Passover each year, which includes eating the Passover lamb to commemorate Israel's deliverance from slavery in Egypt (Luke 2:41; 22:15; John 2:13): "seven days you shall eat with [the lamb] unleavened bread" (Deuteronomy 16:1–3).

Second, *Jesus miraculously multiplied fish (animals!) for large crowds on at least two occasions.* His miraculous feeding of the 5,000 with fish and bread is recorded in all four Gospels; the biblical text affirms that the people ate "of the fish as much as they wanted" (John 6:11)—with twelve baskets of food left over. On another occasion, he fed fish and bread to 4,000 (Matthew 15; Mark 8).

Third, *Jesus helped others secure meat to eat, and he ate meat himself—even in his resurrected state.* When Jesus called the fisherman Simon Peter, this event involved a miraculous catch of animals—*fish* (Luke 5:4–7). Notice that when Jesus called fishermen—Peter and his brother Andrew as well as James and John, the sons of Zebedee (Matthew 4:18–22)—he did not command them to "leave your life of sin." Catching fish was a legitimate vocation. On another occasion, Jesus told Peter to catch a fish, which presumably could be used for eating. But in the fish's mouth would be a four-drachma coin to pay the temple tax (Matthew 17:23–27). In addition, Jesus affirmed that the good heavenly Father gives good gifts, not bad ones. He illustrates this by speaking of children asking a parent for bread or a fish: no good parent would give a stone or a serpent instead (Matthew 7:7–11).

Some may argue that fish are not technically considered "meat" according to certain modern regulatory (or other) standards; for example, vegetarians of the *pescatarian* variety will include fish in their diet but avoid all other meat. But why think that modern regulatory standards are relevant for inhabitants of first-century Palestine? This is an arbitrary imposition. Clearly Jesus is cooking and eating *animals*. Ultimately, all such trivial distinctions are rendered irrelevant by the fact that Jesus "declared all foods clean" or kosher (Mark 7:19).

Jesus's Teaching Allows for a Wider Array of Meats to Eat

For the ancient Israelites, only *kosher* foods were permitted under the law of Moses (Leviticus 11; Deuteronomy 14)—none of the standard foods you'll find in the best Chinese restaurants, like shrimp, crab, pork, ham, and calamari (squid). In their very diet, national Israel was being reminded that they were to be distinct from the nations around them; they had been set apart to God to bring blessing to all the nations (e.g., Deuteronomy 4:6).

But under the New Covenant through Christ's ministry and redemptive mission, God's people will include more than a representation of ethnic Jews. The new true Israel includes Gentiles as well (Romans 2:28–29; 9:6)—an inter-ethnic body of believers scattered throughout the nations.

So for Jesus, when it comes to eating, *all* foods are "kosher"! He declared "all foods clean" (Mark 7:18–19). Notice this point: *Jesus expands—rather than limits—what the people of God may now eat.* Faithful followers of Christ can happily support those Chinese restaurants! Ultimately, Jesus reminds us that it's not the food that we eat that defiles us. Rather, it's the evil things flowing from the human heart that do (Matthew 15:11, 18–20). Let this serve as a strong word of caution to those claiming that meat-eating is inherently defiling. The Son of God—the Creator of all things (John 1:1–3)—bestows his blessing on meat-eating.

In addition, *Jesus presumed the appropriateness of keeping animals for various uses to benefit humans.* To keep *non*-free-roaming animals in stalls helped make the lives of humans easier and lightened their burdens. This is true throughout the world today as well. Such animal-keeping was an expression of human stewardship (the image of God) over the animal world (Luke 13:15).

Some well-meaning, tender-hearted persons insist that Jesus assumes that animals have "rights." And they appeal right to Jesus himself! After all, even sparrows are valuable to God, who provides for them (Matthew 10:29–31; Luke 12:6). But once again, we shouldn't read something into the text that isn't there. After all, God also "clothes" the *flowers of the field* with beauty (Matthew 6:28–30). Does this mean that *plants* have rights as well? This may not be as farfetched as some may think. Back in 2008, the Swiss "authorities" included plants as "beings" possessing "inherent worth."[7] At any rate, simply because God provides for both *birds* and *plants* (and for *us* as well) doesn't mean that all of these creations of God have identical value.

Commenting on birds, Jesus points out that two sparrows are sold for a "cent" (Matthew 10:29) but that humans are far more valuable than they are. But what were sparrows used for in Jesus's day? They were considered *food for the poor*; they would be sold in the marketplace and eaten.[8] The point Jesus is making is this: If God is aware that sparrows fall, how much more is he aware of you when your life is under threat? The biblical scholar R. T. France comments on Matthew 6:26–30, where Jesus commands his disciples to observe the birds of the air (which God feeds) and the lilies of the field (which God clothes) and thus to trust their heavenly Father, who will all the more provide food and clothing for his children:

While the idea of the "dominion" of humanity over the rest of creation has been seriously abused, especially in recent generations, the contention of some more extreme proponents of animal rights that humanity has no special place in God's order for his world finds little biblical support and is here clearly contradicted. It is interesting to observe that the same assumption with regard to the vegetable creation in v. 30, while equally taken for granted, is less explicitly stated than here.[9]

We should observe that Jesus also told his hearers, "Consider the ravens, for they neither sow nor reap; they have no storeroom nor barn, and yet God feeds them; how much more valuable you are than the birds!" (Luke 12:24). How does God provide for the ravens? By giving them meat to eat. As we've noted in the previous chapter, ravens are omnivores but eat mostly meat. Perhaps we could paraphrase here too: "If God provides meat for the ravens, will he not do so for you, who are much more valuable than they?"

Even when the disciples are going out on their mission, Jesus urges them to eat whatever is offered, which could easily include meat. "Whatever city you enter and they receive you, eat what is set before you" (Luke 10:8). Furthermore, Jesus's own parables include celebrating with the feasting of "my oxen and my fattened livestock" (Matthew 22:4) or the famous "fattened calf" in the Prodigal Son story (Luke 15:23). We have here clear indication that meat-eating is a gift and blessing from God.

What about the charge in the previous chapter that Jesus is more concerned about one human life than 2,000 swine? Well, *it's true!* Swine aren't made in the image of God. As we noted, it was actually the "legion" of demonic beings—evil agents—that were responsible for their demise at "Mount Swine-ai." But Jesus places the focus where it belongs: he tells the formerly oppressed and demonized man to tell others "what great things the Lord has done for you, and how He had mercy on you" (Mark 5:19). To Jesus, people matter far more than animals. So we could paraphrase his words from Luke 12:7 as "Do not be afraid. You are worth more than 2,000 swine."

THE BOOK OF ACTS AND MEAT-EATING

With the beginning and growth of the church in the book of Acts, *Jesus's disciples assume the same meat-eating pattern laid out by Jesus.* Believers in Christ could eat meat—including non-kosher foods—as a blessing from God, although it may have taken some of them a bit longer to get this point. The earliest Jewish Christians spread out to proclaim this good news of Jesus to the Gentiles throughout the Roman Empire. The ancient promise to Abraham (Genesis 12:1–3) was being fulfilled. The "seed" (i.e., descendant) of Abraham—namely, Jesus of Nazareth—would be the channel of this blessing to the world (Romans 4; Galatians 3).

The logic of this message was this: *Gentiles didn't need to become Jewish to be true Christians.* The good news of Jesus is free. Of course, the ancient Israelites were saved by faith (Genesis 15:6; see also Hebrews 11). However, the "old boundary markers" that set ancient Israel apart from the nations—being circumcised, eating kosher foods, and celebrating holy days like Passover—no longer mattered as identity-markers. So it was determined that no Jewish burdens from the law of Moses were to be placed on Gentiles (Acts 15:10, 28). The only qualification was that they remember the customs of Jewish believers so as not to cause unnecessary offense.

To drive home this "all foods are clean" lesson, Jesus spoke to the apostle Peter in a vision (Acts 10:9–16). A sheet was lowered from heaven, filled with all kinds of animals prohibited under Jewish kosher law: "there were in it all kinds of four-footed animals and crawling creatures of the earth and birds of the air." Peter was commanded to rise up, kill, and eat these animals, but he replied, "By no means, Lord, for I have never eaten anything unholy and unclean." Just as Jesus had pronounced all foods clean in Mark 7:19, this message was clearly being reinforced here. The special lesson for Peter was that believing Gentiles were family in Christ. This meant that those Jewish ritual or dietary requirements—and related Jew-Gentile boundary markers—were no longer binding: "What God has cleansed, no longer consider unholy" (Acts 10:15).

As the book of Acts advances, we encounter the Jerusalem council in Acts 15. After Paul and Barnabas returned from their missionary journey, they reported what God was doing among the Gentiles. They conferred with the other apostles, the elders, and the whole Jerusalem church about how to incorporate believing Gentiles into the Christian community, given particular Jewish sensitivities.

Notice that the council never even considered prohibiting meat-eating. The gospel simply doesn't forbid this. But in order to help Jewish and Gentile believers come together as the united people of God, each side needed to pay attention to the particular sensitivities of the other. Those on the *Jewish* side would have to loosen up on restrictions defined by the law of Moses (e.g., non-kosher meat that Gentiles ate was also permissible). And for those on the *Gentile* side, they were to be mindful of Jewish sensitivities by avoiding practices associated with pagan worship: eating idol meat, eating meat with blood in it (Jews drained meat of blood first), eating meat of a strangled animal, and fornication.[10]

This idol meat was associated with pagan worship—although later on, Paul loosened even this requirement about meat once offered to idols:

it was permissible to eat just as long as it had been sold in the marketplace. To eat it during pagan temple rituals was another matter since the sacrifices there were an offering to demons (1 Corinthians 8:7–13; 10:20).

One final scene to consider is in Acts 21:26. There, the apostle Paul made a vow and participated in animal sacrifice in the temple, where he had gone to offer "the sacrifice" (see Acts 21:26). This procedure was known as a Nazirite vow, which involved *sacrificing lambs and rams* (Numbers 6:14–17). But why this sacrifice, if Christ had fulfilled the Jewish sacrificial system once for all through his own death (Hebrews 7:27; 9:12; 10:10)? The answer is this: *in light of a certain strong nationalistic feeling in Jerusalem, Paul took precautions to accommodate Jews who thought that Christians didn't care about the law of Moses.* His temple sacrifice was not a moment of weakness—a theological capitulation to Jewish pressure. After all, Paul later made an official "defense," and he specifically referred back to his participation in this event as fully justified and emphasized his endeavoring to live with a "blameless conscience" (Acts 24:10–12, 16–18). He symbolically showed that he wasn't hostile to Jewish traditions—a point he made clear in 1 Corinthians 9; there he said he was a Jew to the Jews and a Gentile to the Gentiles (those without the law of Moses). He contextualized his message in hopes that each might find salvation. So as a Jesus-follower, Paul showed he could still engage in animal sacrifices in the temple even though they were no longer necessary.[11] Even after Christ's death and resurrection, Peter and John went to the temple for the mid-afternoon Jewish prayer time (Acts 3:1)—even though the temple was no longer necessary for Jewish worship since all believers in Christ are the temple of God's Spirit (1 Corinthians 6:19; Revelation 3:12).

PAUL'S WRITINGS

In our final section, we expound further on the apostle Paul's teachings on eating meat. Consider the commentary of Anglican priest and theologian Andrew Linzey on this matter. He takes the view that "to stand with Jesus is to reject our view of ourselves as gods and lords of creation. We are to honor life for the sake of the Lord of life." He adds that "to stand for Jesus is to stand for active compassion for the weak, against the principle that might is right." To justify his position, he quotes the apostle Paul (from Colossians 3:12), who exhorts us to "put on a heart of compassion, kindness, humility." This, he argues, includes our relationship to animals.[12]

Much like the "Veggie Tale" examples in the previous chapter, Linzey's treatment of Scripture on this point is quite *selective.* Indeed, Jesus—the "Lord of life"—permitted eating *every* kind of food, kosher and non-kosher, and he himself ate animal meat. And here in Colossians, Paul has just denounced the local false teachers, who make rules like "Do not handle! Do not taste! Do not touch!" Paul rejects the false spirituality behind prohibitions against eating or drinking certain things: "Therefore no one is to act as your judge in regard to food or drink" (Colossians 2:16; see 1 Timothy 4:1–5). This pseudo-piety about food and drink has "the appearance of wisdom in self-made religion," but it is "of no value against fleshly indulgence" (Colossians 2:23).

Furthermore, Linzey's claim ignores what Paul says in Romans 14 and 1 Corinthians 8 and 10, that those who feel free or strong in "faith"— that is, in their conscience—"may eat all things" (Romans 14:2). Even so, those who recognize their freedom in Christ ("the strong" [Romans 15:1]) *shouldn't look down on* the one who "eats vegetables only" (including Linzey) because he doesn't feel the liberty to eat meat ("the weak"). Paul was "convinced in the Lord Jesus that nothing is unclean in itself" (Romans 14:14). Following the teaching of Jesus, Paul writes, "All things are indeed clean" (Romans 14:20).

Paul was aware that Jewish Christians might have had qualms about eating idol meat from pagan temples—meat that was later sold in the open market. So he declared that eating this market meat was morally permissible if one's conscience permitted it. For the strong in conscience, he said, "Eat anything that is sold in the meat market without asking questions for conscience' sake" (1 Corinthians 10:25). Yet Paul reminded his congregation that "food will not commend us to God; we are neither the worse if we do not eat, nor the better if we do eat" (1 Corinthians 8:8). This is a far cry from the prescriptive vegetarians, who declare that we *are* worse off if we eat meat! Even as an apostle, Paul had "a right to eat and drink" (1 Corinthians 9:4)—just as those who served in the temple could eat meat and other foods presented at the altar (1 Corinthians 9:13–14). Since the earth is the Lord's and everything in it (1 Corinthians 10:25–26), Paul told believers that they were free to eat meat so long as it wasn't connected to the rituals of pagan worship.

We have already noted a key text of Paul's—1 Timothy 4:1–5. Paul denounced those who "forbid marriage and advocate abstaining from foods which God has created to be gratefully shared in by those who believe and know the truth." These are "doctrines of demons" propounded by hypocritical "liars." This is very strong language against those who prohibit the good gifts of God—sex within marriage and *all* things edible. And Paul assumed that *from the outset of creation* God created all these things to be enjoyed by human beings and "received with gratitude." Meat-eating was blessed from the very beginning—*not* as a result of the fall.

The prescriptive Christian vegetarian might reluctantly acknowledge that the "Bible does not prohibit eating meat in all circumstances," as does the Christian Vegetarian Association pamphlet noted in the last chapter.[13]

But that's a very misleading way of putting it. The pamphlet should read, "The Bible pronounces—in *abundance*—blessing on meat-eating, which is a gift from a generous God." But then the pamphlet adds that the Edenic "plant-based diet as God's ideal" is what was predicted by prophets (e.g., Isaiah 11:6–9), who foresaw "a return to this harmonious world."[14]

Let's review what we noted in the last chapter—and again keep in mind that this is one Christian perspective of several that could be presented in response to prescriptive Christian vegetarianism. We pointed out that this original vegetarianism doesn't square with other biblical texts. Creation's animal food chain is called "good" (Psalm 104:28). We also noted that Isaiah 25:6 foresees a final state in which the redeemed will enjoy "the best of meats and the finest of wines" (NIV). What's more, the "lion with the lamb" scenario is just a picture of peace and tranquility. After all, Isaiah later says "no lion will be there" (Isaiah 35:9) to lie down with the lamb! So which do we take literally—feasting on fine meats, lion with lamb, or no lion at all?

Now for the sake of argument, let's just say that eating meat will be done away with in the new creation. Of course, the new creation has already begun with Christ's bodily resurrection (see 2 Corinthians 5:17; Galatians 6:15)—what the theologian Irenaeus called "the eighth day of creation." A common prescriptive Christian vegetarian assertion is that we should therefore comply with this "new creation ethic" *now* by stopping all meat-eating.

There are at least three problems here: First, *after Jesus's bodily resurrection (the new creation's beginning), he nevertheless ate fish (animals) in this new, glorified condition!* Second, if we follow that logic of "let's stop eating meat now," then we should forbid marriage as well. We can ask, *Since marriage won't be part of the new heavens and new earth either (Mark 12:25), why even get married?* Shouldn't we begin living the alleged "ideal" now? If we admit that marriage has a vital place for humanity up until the new heavens and earth arrive (as part of the "dominion" task), then the "dominion" of meat-eating should also be included up until the very end. Third, *Paul actually condemned those who teach that vegetarianism is inherently more spiritual than meat-eating; he said such a teaching belongs to what he pronounced "doctrines of demons"* (1 Timothy 4:1–5). This is a very serious charge that the more strident of prescriptive Christian vegetarians should note.

Various Christians will hold up models of "animal compassion" such as Francis of Assisi or abolitionist William Wilberforce, who was concerned about animal cruelty (e.g., dog-fighting, bull-baiting). We can certainly applaud the latter's efforts to correct abuses of human stewardship and causing pointless animal pain. However, we can do so *without* affirming animal rights and also without denying the permissibility of meat-eating. *We must not be more spiritual than the Bible—or more than Christ himself, who declared all foods clean.*

CONCLUSION

In this chapter, we have observed that the Christian faith is a knowledge tradition. This means we have *two* sources of knowledge. First is God's *general* revelation to all, which includes philosophical reasons for affirming human uniqueness and rejecting the notion of animal "rights" (see chapters 5 and 6). Second is God's *special* revelation in Scripture, which furnishes us with resources to speak knowledgeably about the permissibility of meat-eating. Indeed, these Scriptures are a matter of public truth, not mere private piety that is more akin to personal opinion or preference. Rather, we can know with confidence that God has spoken through Jesus Christ, who taught that all foods are clean. He and the rest of the New Testament authorities reject—and even denounce—those who teach prescriptive Christian vegetarianism as more spiritual than meat-eating. No, eating meat is a gift from God that is to be received with thanksgiving. Matters of conscience are one thing. But those proclaiming the prohibition of "do not handle, do not taste, do not touch" meat of any kind (Colossians 2:21) go beyond merely being "weaker" in faith to actually being *anti-spiritual* and standing in opposition to the entire testimony of Scripture.

PART V
WHY THIS MATTERS FOR YOU

10. Scripture and Swine: Does Scripture Allow Me to Raise Pigs for Food?

GORDON SPRONK AND RANDY SPRONK

You put us in charge of your handcrafted world,
repeated to us your Genesis-charge, Made us lords of sheep
and cattle, even animals out in the wild.
(Psalm 8:6, MSG)

The theologian feeds the soul, the philosopher feeds the mind,
the agriculturist feeds the world and he uses the
blessings of his labors ... meat.
(Gordon Spronk)

OUR FAMILY BACKGROUND

Humanity eats food, including meat. We are creative spirits intended to worship God, say prayers of thanks before we eat, break bread together, and accept food (including meat) as a gift from God. The family table where we have gathered for generations enforces the basic spiritual concepts of family, hearts of gratitude, and our creative purpose. Families that eat together create villages. Villages create countries, and countries create civilizations.

Our family has relied on agriculture as a career for generations. With no formal education in the past, you learned animal husbandry at the feet of your father and grandfather. Today, our family has individuals with degrees—some with advanced degrees—in animal science, animal husbandry, business administration, veterinary health and medicine, epidemiology, animal diseases, meat science, zoonotic disease transmission, and more. Yet, we cannot recall one class that taught us *the spiritual or theological* aspect of food production or raising animals for food. Could it be that while more educated, we are less wise? It is possible that while more educated we are currently overwhelmed by a culture based on secular understanding with no clear answers to life's greatest questions. Members of our family for more than sixteen generations were *called to feed the world by raising livestock* using God-given talents, skills, and assets. Is this a kingdom calling? We believe it is.

Being raised on a farm, caring for animals every day (or twice a day and more), and relying on them for your income give rise to an entirely different relationship than does the care and feeding of the dogs and other pets we own. Feeding the hungry, clothing the naked, and taking care of the widow and orphan are *the least* we are called to do if we have entered into the kingdom of the Heavens as disciples of Jesus Christ. We begin with this foundational understanding of reality that may not be the same starting point for all and where we may be on a different path than some others in the world.

Agriculturists have sustained civilizations for millennia through raising food in the form of meat and vegetables. Farmers have freed humanity from the daily burden of gathering vegetables and hunting meat to allow the God-given skills of technology, education, and culture to be released upon the earth; *divinely-mandated stewardship of animals and dominion of the earth allow this.* We believe this activity is all included in the prayer "your kingdom come, your will be done" (Matthew 6:10, NIV).

Now, some will raise a *spiritual* argument for a separation of agriculture into vegetable raising (good) and raising of animals for food (bad). But a study of Scripture reveals this is a nonissue. Until recently, students of Scripture never considered this matter, nor has it been widely discussed in any currently available agricultural or theological curricula. Why is that? Could it be that critics of the modern food system are now co-opting *any argument*—including purportedly biblical ones and the *"What would Jesus do?"* question—to frame criticism of how food is raised and what we should eat today? Why is the center of the plate under attack now? On what is our spiritual, emotional, intellectual, and physical relationship to animals based? Is it the identical relationship we have with our family pets?

SOME AGRICULTURE BACKGROUND

The concept of agriculture is simple: those with superior agricultural skills raise more food than is needed for their family, and the excess food is then sold to those who need food. This transactional exchange can only occur if buyer and seller agree that the food is abundant, safe, healthy, economical, and nutritious. This economic exchange is basic: excess food from our farm is exchanged for your commercial goods, with the result of improvement for society and the farmer. Both are allowed to advance. The better for the farmer, the bigger the crop. The better for the animal caretaker, the more productive the animals. Travel the world today, and you will find that the richest (most blessed?) areas of the globe have some basic attributes in common: rich soil, favorable climate (rain), and animal caretakers with a high degree of sophistication, technology, and *spiritual awareness* of their stewardship calling.

It is of interest that for millennia, *the spiritual aspect* of agriculture—specifically, raising animals for meat consumption, keeping livestock in controlled environments, production of more with less (more bushels per acre or more pigs per sow per year)—has been uplifted and upheld *from a spiritual standpoint.*

"The LORD is my shepherd" is a prime example of the Bible using an agricultural relationship to stake a foundational claim that animal care is paramount. As disciples of Christ Jesus, we also rely spiritually and physically on this promise: "I have a shepherd. I lack nothing." This foundational passage sends a message directly to any caretakers of their stewardship responsibilities while remaining silent on why animals were in a flock in the first place: to provide food and clothing. This may provide clues to the concerns raised: What is the proper relationship of a human being to an animal? Simply put, in our current culture, this discussion quickly divides into two distinct thought camps—especially in an American culture where billions of dollars are spent annually on pets, and less than 2 percent of the population lives on a farm:

We have animals (pets) that we care for, *but we do not eat them.*
We have animals (livestock) we *care for*, with the primary purpose to provide food: *we eat them.*

Spiritual questions raised in recent decades by academics, theologians, and philosophers are not raised in a vacuum (or with empty stomachs). Rather, they are raised in tandem with trends *of more food than ever*, more people than ever, and more information than ever. This all culminates in the growing movement in our culture of *how we eat*. A culture of pleasure, instant gratification, consumerism, and freedom creates an environment with a potent mix of cute, clever, and cunning subcultures of pleasure and freedom, whose motives may not be readily discernible, while allowing everyone to *"have it your way."* Is there so much freedom now that we are allowed to *"have it our way"* in the *spiritual* dimension also? We leave it to the theologians and philosophers to sort that out; this chapter focuses on raising animals for food.

The leap to a *spiritual conclusion* that raising food and meat is beneficial may be simple: when confronted with hunger, should we not solve it?

Is there less thought placed on how food is raised when faced with the question "Do we have any food?" Are we asking these questions of the *spiritual foundation* of raising animals and eating meat only when food is affordable, abundant, and safe in a way unheard of in the entirety of humanity? In the history of the world when millions have died of famine and hunger (take your pick of natural disasters or misplaced government mandates) was the question ever asked "Is it spiritually correct (for humans to eat meat)?" Economists have ably documented that human development is consistent in one thing: as soon as people have more than a certain threshold of money in their pocket, the intake and variety of food goes up (and the demand for meat rises). Is this desire human or from God?

It goes unstated that King David, who was once a shepherd boy, was taking care of sheep that were being raised for one primary purpose—*to eat them*. Although he wrote Psalm 23 to describe the divine shepherd who provides for and protects his flock, David knew that sheep generally are not pets. While the Old Testament does give one pet-like approximation (2 Samuel 12:3), the Scriptures remain silent on their purpose and care. "The Lord takes care of His pets" does not have the same ring to it and has an entirely different meaning.

Scripture goes even further when describing the opposite of having a shepherd (I have everything I need) when describing desolation in the form of disease, death, and famine (lack of food):

> Though the fig tree should not blossom
> And there be no fruit on the vines,
> Though the yield of the olive should fail
> And the fields produce no food,
> Though the flock should be cut off from the fold
> And there be no cattle in the stalls,
> Yet I will exult in the LORD,
> I will rejoice in the God of my salvation. (Habakkuk 3:17–18)

To clarify, flocks and herds have a purpose: to feed the hungry, to be eaten.

Grandpa taught us the basics of animal care, husbandry, and economics. Land-grant universities taught us the advancements of science and technology. We have traveled the world to observe agriculture in Europe, Central and South America, and Asia, and our education continues to this day. This family history and education provide an interesting perspective on food production and its evolution regardless of spiritual knowledge. In Asia, for example, little thought is given to how animals are raised, cared for, or slaughtered: the population simply wants food—indeed, *meat*—to eat.

The region in northern Europe where our great grandparents lived is still used for agriculture and raising livestock—specifically, swine. The basic knowledge of animal husbandry—the care and raising of animals—starts with practical hands-on knowledge of individual animal care. Animals need daily food, water, and a place to eat and sleep protected from predators and the environment. In some cultures, swine are favored for three basic reasons: they will eat nearly anything (table scraps); they are reproductively efficient (one sow mated will produce a litter of pigs); and the meat satisfies both taste and nutritional needs, not to mention the added benefits that every last part of a pig is used. Intestinal tracts are used for sausage casings; pharmaceuticals are derived from glands; and consumer products are made from bones and skin. In fact, today pork is the most consumed meat in the world (you can even eat the feet) due to the many resources that come from a pig.

How pigs are cared for has changed through the generations. Grandfather raised swine outdoors in unheated huts with straw bedding and hand-feeding. In some cultures, pigs are herded; in others they live in a housing compound. Over time, pigs were moved from outdoor pens to inside housing as we learned more about their specific nutritional and environmental needs. Today, the entire life cycle of the pig is completely different than just one generation ago. In the past, sows were mated twice per year—once in the spring, once in the fall—and 114 days later a litter was born, and 200 days after that, pigs were ready to be slaughtered for consumption.

Today, while the biology is the same, there have been many advancements in nutrition, housing, and care. By every measure, things have improved for the pig. The diet they eat is no longer left over from other activities. The water they drink equals the quality for human consumption, and they are housed in controlled environments with temperature and air quality to meet their needs. They have accommodations that are superior to millions of humans. Disease is controlled with immunity management, and pathogen transmission is prevented as much as possible to preserve the health of these animals. The daily care meets the needs of the pig, and the results are astounding by many measures: The amount of meat produced today compared to our grandfathers' day and as measured by pounds per sow per year has more than doubled to over two and a half tons. The pigs are healthier by many measures: no parasites, no viruses, and fewer bacteria. Life is better. Our creative will has been used! Is it possible to conclude that we "have dominion" over the raising of swine? How does one *measure* dominion?

How we raise pigs changed, and society has also changed. We no longer are an agrarian culture. In fact, less than 2 percent of our population in the United States now lives on a farm. In other words, 98 percent of our population is more than one generation away from hands-on experience of how their food is raised. This disconnect between the farm and the table may provide some insight into the kinds of questions some may ask of us:

The "care" concern: How do we treat our animals?
The "save Mother Earth" concern: How is the manure that the pigs generate disposed of?
The "what is good?" concern: A question Christians should be asking is How do we feed the hungry?

These questions have answers if we are allowed the opportunity to answer them. Yes, our pigs are well cared for! They have free access to food, water, and air twenty-four hours a day, seven days a week. The manure is an asset to a land-based system that is sustainable: the pigs generate the manure; the manure contains nearly the exact profile for production of corn and soybeans; and those crops are nearly exactly the nutritional profile the pig needs. This loop of corn to pigs to manure back to soil to corn has increased soil health and tilth. Today we can use science to measure this via life cycle assessments and carbon footprint calculators. By all measures over the last 50 years (our father's generation to our generation), our land, water, and carbon footprint have been improved and enhanced.

So, if practical observation says this works—more pigs per sow, more corn per acre, more meat produced—what does science say? By any measure of efficiency, we have "dominion": the rate of growth (average daily gain), the amount of feed fed (feed efficiency), health (mortality rate), and cost (the cost of meat compared to percentage of daily wage). And success on many levels as measured by output, efficiency, repeatability, and throughput leads us back to where we started: *Is this spiritually correct?*

A disclaimer: we are pig farmers, not theologians. We know a lot about raising livestock; we know the subtleties of which corn variety is favored, which breed has which attribute, which way a pig will turn when approached from behind, the volume and value of the manure generated; and we know that pork tastes good (especially bacon). So, although other chapters in this book address the direct spiritual question from different angles, we only answer this from a personal perspective. What are we called to do? Where do we gain insight and *spiritual guidance?* Our answer is direct: we are called to discipleship in God's eternally creative kingdom, and we gain insight by reading his Word as we seek.

DISCIPLES DISGUISED AS PIG FARMERS

As we understand from Scripture, *Spirit (or spirit) is an animating personal power*. We are being asked to respond to what we do in a spiritual context. The Bible says that God is spirit and that he acts. Where God acts, his action reveals something of his kingdom—where what he wants done is done: "Your kingdom come. Your will be done." We can only apply this prayer, this action, this calling to our lives. This will, of God, to be done in my life—*that is my calling*.

So, as we understand it, *a spiritual life* is a life lived from the direction, power, motivation, character, and leading of Jesus himself. Christ in me gives me *a spiritual life*. Jesus is joined in this relationship (a Trinitarian relationship) by God the Father and the Holy Spirit. If we live this life, it will be a life lived in the power of the resurrected life of Jesus. Can a pig farmer live this life? How does this apply to a life raising livestock for food and meat? We can only rely further on Scripture to gain insight into *this spiritual life* we are called to live.

In Matthew 6:33, Jesus is talking about something important as he begins his ministry. He starts out with something very simple, available to all, and radical: "Seek first His kingdom and His righteousness, and all these things will be added to you." All my concerns—including whether I should eat meat or raise pigs—are captured here. If I just *do this one thing*, everything else is taken care of. Note that it says *seek*, not *find*. This is important since what I seek defines my life, my thoughts, my actions, and my motives, including eating food and eating meat. *Seeking bends my will* to finding until I have success. I seek everywhere until I find. I seek to find the kingdom of God and his righteousness; I seek to find God in action. Where do I look? *Everywhere*—including on my farm and in my pig barns.

Beyond this, we find other Scriptures that promise God's provision if we take care of *just this one thing*—to make God's priorities our own.

Psalm 23, which we referenced earlier in this chapter, states, "The LORD is my shepherd. I shall not want."[1] The world places many demands upon us, and life can appear threatening. I realize that I cannot deal with all of this on my own, including what I eat or whether I should eat meat or raise animals for food. However, when I seek God's kingdom first, these kinds of things fall into place. I find the kingdom and its righteousness include all the daily farming decisions that attach to me the moment I rise from bed in the morning. I can confidently rely on this simple thing I am called to do. Why does God do it this way? Why has he not made this immediately obvious? Why did God not make life's demands and complexities simple?

This is how I understand it: *What I seek* shows what I am; *our wants or pursuits reveal who we are.* What do I seek? What is my life really about? Beyond my vocation, beyond death, what do I seek? What I seek reflects an effort to pull my life together, and it makes my life what it is. As human beings, we are left free to choose what we want. But what will I say when I stand before God? Did I really need more evidence whether to eat meat or not to eat meat? My choices make me who I am. What do I seek?

These are sobering questions. Thankfully, Scripture provides more guidance. In Jeremiah 29:13, God tells his people, "You will seek Me and find Me when you search for Me with all your heart." My selfish wants are very distinct from God's will. I oppose his kingdom with my kingdom. But this is Jesus's gospel: "Repent, for the kingdom of heaven is at hand" (Matthew 3:2), to me, to all. The kingdom of heaven—God's rule—has broken into history and is available right here, right now. It is available to everyone—to anyone who simply looks at him and trusts him. No longer do I depend on others, or my works, to gain salvation. Even pig farmers can answer this call to submit to the rule of God's kingdom. This gospel makes clear that those who are so far down on the scale of life (including pig farmers) qualify because they acknowledge their need.

Other biblical texts remind me of this. Heeding God's ways leads to God's approval and blessing (Joshua 1:8). *My life as a farmer cannot guarantee me what these verses guarantee me.* Psalm 1 speaks of something similar: those who are well-rooted in God's Word—those who do "not live by bread alone" (Deuteronomy 8:3)—will exhibit lives of stability, substance, and fruitfulness (Psalm 1:1–4). Similarly, Proverbs 3:5–6 applies to the spiritual life of the farmer who will trust in God and acknowledge him in all his ways—that is, he expects God to be involved in everything he is doing. This means that I cannot be wise in my own eyes even as an agriculturalist/farmer. God calls me to clothe myself in humility and to humble myself under God's mighty hand so that he may exalt me at the proper time (1 Peter 5:5–7). In humbling myself, I must be realistic about myself and the task of farming. I cannot manage this on my own. Only with God's help will this life work, even as a humble pig farmer.

CLOSING THOUGHTS

"The hand of God" often suggests God in action: If we depend on him, if we acknowledge him, he will exalt us in his time. He wants this for us even more than we, parents and grandparents, seek to exalt our children and grandchildren. We simply begin where we are. Then we will know the fullness *of a spiritual life* if we stay on this path—beginning where we are, seeking first the kingdom of God and his righteousness. If we stay on this path, we will know *the full life of the Spirit, even as pig farmers.* These are simple lessons intended to bring glory to Jesus and his cause.

Raising animals for meat is a spiritual calling in response to the command to take our place in God's kingdom. Each of us has his or her own calling in this kingdom. This is ours to seek and find. As his disciples, we do these things as we seek and bend our desire in order to do God's will, to do what is good. And what is good some call love, and since God is love, we do it out of love for the entire earth. That is our understanding of how to use our creative will, moving in concert with God's kingdom.[2]

ENDNOTES

1. YOU ARE WHAT YOU SAY YOU EAT BY THOMAS J. ST. ANTOINE

1. Richard Weaver, *The Ethics of Rhetoric* (Davis: Hermagoras Press, 1985), 17.
2. Eric Schlosser, *Fast Food Nation: The Dark Side of the All-American Meal* (New York: Perennial, 2002).
3. *Super Size Me: A Film of Epic Proportions*, directed by Morgan Spurlock, performed by Morgan Spurlock and Alexandra Jamieson, The Con Production Company, 2004, film.
4. See Michael Pollan, *In Defense of Food: An Eater's Manifesto* (New York: Penguin, 2008); or *The Omnivore's Dilemma: A Natural History of Four Meals* (New York: Penguin, 2006).
5. *Food, Inc.*, directed by Robert Kenner and Elise Pearlstein, performed by Eric Schlosser and Michael Pollan, Magnolia Pictures, 2008, film.
6. Paul Roberts, *The End of Food* (Boston: Mariner, 2009).
7. Hank Cardello and Douglas Garr, *Stuffed: An Insider's Look at Who's (Really) Making America Fat* (New York: CCC, 2009).
8. Jayson Lusk, *The Food Police: A Well-Fed Manifest About the Politics of Your Plate* (New York: Crown Forum, 2013).
9. "Faith Outreach," Humane Society of the United States, accessed March 22, 2019, https://www.humanesociety.org/resources/hsus-faith-councils.
10. "Facts and Faith: Religious Statements on Animals," Humane Society of the United States, accessed March 22, 2019, https://www.humanesociety.org/resources/facts-and-faith.
11. "Every Living Thing," accessed March 22, 2019, www.everylivingthing.com/sign-the-statement/.

12. Walter Fisher, *Human Communication as Narration: Toward a Philosophy of Reason, Value and Action* (Columbia: University of South Carolina Press, 1987).
13. The author wishes to thank Don Keller for his helpful comments on these first two chapters.

2. BASIC INGREDIENTS BY THOMAS J. ST. ANTOINE

1. These agrarian images are too numerous to list in this short volume. They include, for example, Christ as shepherd and Christ's parables and sayings that appeal to sowing, pruning, and harvesting. These examples emerged from a culture that, itself, was largely agrarian.
2. Michael Pollan, *The Omnivore's Dilemma: A Natural History of Four Foods* (New York: Penguin, 2006), 137.
3. *A Pig's Tail*, Humane Society of the United States, March 22, 2019, https://www.youtube.com/watch?v=pr7jqcVRA94. This animation invokes the popular practice in pop culture of personifying farm animals in Disney films and other popular family films, such as *Babe, Charlotte's Web, Home on the Range,* and *Barnyard.*
4. "Facts and Faith: Religious Statements on Animals," Humane Society of the United States, accessed March 22, 2019, https://www.humanesociety.org/resources/facts-and-faith.
5. Hank Cardello and Douglas Garr, *Stuffed: An Insider's Look at Who's (Really) Making America Fat* (New York: CCC, 2009), 94.
6. Distrust of the food industry can also be seen in the American literary tradition—for example, Upton Sinclair's novel *The Jungle.*
7. *Food, Inc.*, directed by Robert Kenner and Elise Pearlstein, performed by Eric Schlosser and Michael Pollan, Magnolia Pictures, 2008, film.
8. Wendell Berry, *What Are People For?* (Berkeley: Counterpoint, 2010), 146.
9. Berry, *What Are People For?*, 148.
10. See Matthew Regier, "Jacques Ellul and Wendell Berry on an Agrarian Resistance," *Ellul Forum,* 46 (Fall 2012): 17.
11. Pollan, *Omnivore's Dilemma*, 158.
12. Pollan, *Omnivore's Dilemma*, 118.
13. Berry, *What Are People For?*, 151.
14. "Faith Outreach," Humane Society of the United States, accessed March 22, 2019, https://www.humanesociety.org/faith-outreach.
15. "Every Living Thing," accessed March 22, 2019, www.everylivingthing.com/sign-the-statement/.
16. "Every Living Thing."
17. "Every Living Thing."
18. "Episcopal Church," Humane Society of the United States, August 2012, https://www.humanesociety.org/sites/default/files/docs/episcopal-church-factsheet.pdf.
19. "Eric Metaxas: William Wilberforce & Animals Part 2 of 4," Humane Society of the United States, accessed April 8, 2019, https://www.youtube.com/watch?v=OD1qkIHUmHk.

20. "An Evangelical Statement on Responsible Care for Animals: Explanatory Essay," accessed April 8, 2019, http://www.everylivingthing.com/wp-content/uploads/2015/09/An-Evangelical-Statement-on-Responsible-Care-for-Animals_Explanatory-Essay1.pdf.

21. "The United Methodist Church," Humane Society of the United States, accessed April 7, 2019, https://www.humanesociety.org/sites/default/files/docs/united-methodist-church-factsheet.pdf.

22. Edward Pentin, "Iraqi Orthodox Bishop: The West Cares More About Frogs Than Us," *The National Catholic Register*, April 7, 2017, http://www.ncregister.com/blog/edward-pentin/iraqi-orthodox-bishop-the-west-cares-more-about-frogs-than-us.

23. Ovid, *The Metamorphoses*, trans. A. D. Melville (New York: Oxford, 2008), 4, 5.

24. "Every Living Thing."

25. "The Roman Catholic Church," The Humane Society of the United States, accessed April 8, 2019, https://www.humanesociety.org/sites/default/files/docs/roman-catholic-church-factsheet-revised.pdf.

26. "Every Living Thing."

27. "An Evangelical Statement on Responsible Care for Animals."

28. Berry, *What Are People For?*, 152.

3. PIGS, PEAS, AND SEALS: THE UNIVERSALITY OF MEAT-EATING

BY WES JAMISON

1. M. Titcomb, *Dog and Man in the Ancient Pacific* (Honolulu: Bishop Press, 1969).

2. Matthew Scully, *Dominion: The Power of Man, the Suffering of Animals, and the Call to Mercy* (New York: St. Martin's Griffin Press, 2003).

3. "Dominion" comes from Genesis 1:26, where God gives people the right to rule over animals, like vice-regents (with God) who are given permission to use animals—yes, wisely—for their own benefit. The *imago Dei* is a theological term that notes that only humans are created in God's image, and thus they are truly unique.

4. JOY OR GRIEF? UNDERSTANDING THE CHALLENGES TO CHRISTIAN MEAT-EATING BY WES JAMISON

1. Alex Prichard, *Justice, Order and Anarchy: The International Political Theory of Pierre-Joseph Proudhon* (London: Routledge, 2013).

2. Martin E. Marty, *Politics, Religion, and the Common Good* (San Francisco: Jossey-Bass, 2000).

3. D. Stonehouse, "'Godfather' of animal rights out to counter Christianity: Belief that humans are superior to all other beings is promoted through Bible teachings, ethicist argues," *The Ottawa Citizen* (July 5, 2002), A1.

4. Personal communication (February 24, 2019).

5. John Hare, "Animal Sacrifices," in *Divine Evil?: The Moral Character of the God of Abraham*, eds. Michael Bergmann et al. (New York: Oxford University Press, 2011), 136.

6. Stephen Vantassel and Nelson Kloosterman, "Compassionate Eating as Distortion of Scripture: Using Religion to Serve Food Morality," *Evangelical Review of Society and Politics* 5, no. 1 (2011): 34–35.

7. Matthew Scully, *Dominion: The Power of Man, the Suffering of Animals, and the Call to Mercy* (New York: St. Martin's Griffin Press, 2003).

8. See Michael Murray, *Nature Red in Tooth and Claw: Theism and the Problem of Animal Suffering* (New York: Oxford University Press, 2008).

9. Matthew Scully, "Fear Factories: The Case for Compassionate Conservatism—for Animals," *The American Conservative*, May 23, 2005, https://www.theamericanconservative.com/articles/fear-factories/.

10. Matthew C. Halteman, *Compassionate Eating as Care of Creation* (Washington: Humane Society, 2010), 6. Available at https://www.humanesociety.org/sites/default/files/docs/compassionate-eating-halteman-book.pdf. Note: I have slightly edited the quotation here, changing the unwieldy poetic rendering to more manageable prose.

11. Vantassel and Kloosterman, "Compassionate Eating," 45.

12. Harold O. J. Brown, "Of Animal and Human Rights," *Christian Research Journal* (April 20, 2009). Available at https://www.equip.org/article/of-animal-and-human-rights/.

5. THERE IS NOTHING MORALLY WRONG WITH EATING MEAT
BY TIMOTHY HSIAO

1. For example, the animal rights organization PETA (People for the Ethical Treatment of Animals) is well known for its campaigns that equate meat production and consumption to murder. One such campaign even equated modern agricultural practices to the Holocaust. Other examples are documented in Wesley J. Smith, *A Rat Is a Pig Is a Dog Is a Boy: The Human Costs of the Animal Rights Movement* (New York: Encounter, 2012).

2. The two most influential works on this front are Tom Regan, *The Case for Animal Rights* (Berkeley: University of California Press, 1983); and Peter Singer, *Animal Liberation*, 3rd ed. (New York: Cambridge University Press, 2011). Other philosophers, including James Rachels, David DeGrazia, Alastair Norcross, and Mylan Engel, have made similar arguments that build on Regan and Singer.

3. Interested readers may also consult Timothy Hsiao, "In Defense of Eating Meat," *Journal of Agricultural and Environmental Ethics* 28, no. 2 (2015): 277–291; and "Industrial Farming Is Not Cruel to Animals," *Journal of Agricultural and Environmental Ethics* 30, no. 1 (2017): 37–54.

4. The account of moral status and rights that I am defending here is a version of natural law theory. Readers who are interested in learning more about natural law should see Brian Besong, *An Introduction to Ethics: A Natural Law Approach* (Eugene: Wipf and Stock, 2018). For a specifically Christian introduction, see David Haines and Andrew Fulford, *Natural Law: A Brief Introduction and Biblical Defense* (Lincoln: The Davenant Trust, 2017).

5. This is developed in greater detail in David S. Oderberg, *Moral Theory: A Non Consequentialist Approach* (Oxford: Blackwell, 2000).

6 Many within the Judeo-Christian tradition have historically understood the image of God in terms of possessing such a nature.

7. Russell DiSilvestro, *Human Capacities and Moral Status* (New York: Springer, 2010), 10–12.

8. James Reichmann, *Evolution, Animal 'Rights,' and the Environment* (Washington: Catholic University of America Press, 2000).

9. What about beginning-of-life scenarios, where there appears to be controversy over whether preborn humans possess rights? Even here, many pro-choice philosophers do not argue that preborn humans completely lack rights or moral status. The claim is rather that they possess these things to a lesser degree or that their interests are outweighed by the interests of another party.

10. The late Tom Regan, who is regarded as one of the academic founding fathers of the modern animal rights movement, argued that animals have rights because they have a set of cognitive properties that makes them "subjects-of-a-life." None of the cognitive properties he lists, however, bear on the kind of rationality necessary for possessing moral status. For a detailed critique of Regan, see David S. Oderberg, *Applied Ethics: A Non-Consequentialist Approach* (Oxford: Blackwell, 2000), chapter 3.

11. See Marie George, "Thomas Aquinas Meets Nim Chimpsky: On the Debate About Human Nature and the Nature of Other Animals," *The Aquinas Review* 10 (2000): 1–50; and Reichmann, *Evolution, Animal 'Rights,' and the Environment*.

12. Mylan Engel, "The Mere Considerability of Animals," *Acta Analytica* 16 (2001): 89–107; and David DeGrazia, "Moral Vegetarianism from a Very Broad Basis," *Journal of Moral Philosophy* 6, no. 2 (2009): 143–165.

13. For example, James Rachels, "The Basic Argument for Vegetarianism," in *Food for Thought: The Debate Over Eating Meat*, ed. S. Sapontzis (Amherst: Prometheus, 2004), 70–80; Alasdair Norcross, "Puppies, Pigs, and People: Eating Meat and Marginal Cases," *Philosophical Perspectives* 18, 1 (2004): 229–245; Dan Hooley and Nathan Nobis, "A Moral Argument for Veganism," in *Philosophy Comes to Dinner: Arguments on the Ethics of Eating*, eds. A. Chignell, M. Halteman, and T. Cuneo (New York: Routledge, 2015); and Mylan Engel, "The Commonsense Case for Ethical Vegetarianism," *Between the Species* 19, no. 1 (2016): 3–31.

14. See Michael Murray, *Nature Red in Tooth and Claw: Theism and the Problem of Animal Suffering* (Oxford: Oxford University Press, 2008).

15. In online circles, this is sometimes takes the form of the "name the trait" argument.

16. The view that there exist real biological kinds is known as *essentialism*. Some philosophers have attacked this idea as outdated and incompatible with modern science. But this is not true. For robust defenses of essentialism, see David S. Oderberg, *Real Essentialism* (New York: Routledge, 2008); and

Edward Feser, *Aristotle's Revenge: The Metaphysical Foundations of Physical and Biological Science* (Heusenstamm: Editiones Scholasticae, 2019). For a helpful survey of contemporary defenses of essentialism, see Matthew O'Brien and Robert Koons, "Who's Afraid of Metaphysics?," *Public Discourse,* June 2011, https://www.thepublicdiscourse.com/2011/06/3356/.

17. See DiSilvestro, *Human Capacities and Moral Status;* and J. P. Moreland and Scott Rae, *Body and Soul: Human Nature and the Crisis in Ethics* (Downers Grove: IVP Academic, 2000).

18. This way of thinking has significant implications for the way we view abortion. See DiSilvestro, *Human Capacities and Moral Status;* Moreland and Rae, *Body and Soul;* Francis Beckwith, *Defending Life: A Moral and Legal Case Against Abortion Choice* (New York: Cambridge University Press, 2007); and Patrick Lee and Robert P. George, *Body-Self Dualism in Contemporary Ethics and Politics* (New York: Cambridge University Press, 2008).

19. Nor are there what some philosophers call "moral patients." There simply cannot be a moral being that is not in *any* sense capable of pursuing the good. For in what sense would such a being be considered a *moral* being or a member of the *moral* community? Given the nature and purpose of morality, a member of the moral community must possess the capacity to act for moral reasons. Individuals who lack the *developed* capacity for moral agency may be classified as patients in the sense that they are not currently capable of acting for the sake of moral reasons and are thus in a passive state with respect to this ability. Still, the agent-patient distinction is conceptually unhelpful. We are better off speaking in terms of moral agents with differing levels of ability, rather than referring to some agents as patients (which obscures the fact that they possess some degree of agency).

20. See Norcross, "Puppies, Pigs, and People." On a personal note, I once encountered a campus activist from Vegan Outreach who attempted to use this argument against me. My response (which is the same one I offer here) horrified him, much to my amusement.

21. And arguably, the increasing amount of value that is attributed to pets in Western cultures dangerously borders on over-humanizing them in ways that corrupt our moral sensibilities. This can be seen in the tendency of many individuals to treat their pets as if they were children. As Peter Carruthers argues, "the increasing moral importance accorded to animals in our culture can be seen as a form of creeping moral corruption and should be resisted. Particular attention would need to be paid to the moral education of our young." See Peter Carruthers, "Animal Mentality: Its Character, Extent, and Moral Significance," in *The Oxford Handbook of Animal Ethics,* eds. R. Frey and T. Beauchamp (Oxford: Oxford University Press, 2011), 373–406.

22. See Nigel Biggar, *In Defence of War* (Oxford: Oxford University Press, 2014).

23. Readers interested in further critiques of animal rights along broadly natural law lines may consult Carl Cohen, "Do Animals Have Rights?," *Ethics and Behavior* 7, no. 2 (1997): 91–102; Reichmann, *Evolution, Animal 'Rights,' and the Environment*; Oderberg, *Applied Ethics*, chapter 3; Roger Scruton, *Animal Rights and Wrongs*, 3rd ed. (London: Metro and Demos, 2000); Tibor Machan, *Putting Humans First: Why We Are Nature's Favorite* (Lanham: Rowman and Littlefield, 2004); and Hsiao, "In Defense of Eating Meat" and "Industrial Farming Is Not Cruel to Animals." Peter Carruthers offers a critique of animal rights from a contractualist perspective in *The Animals Issue: Moral Theory in Practice* (New York: Cambridge University Press, 1992).

6. HUMAN LIVES MATTER: REFLECTIONS ON HUMAN EXCEPTIONALISM BY TIMOTHY HSIAO

1. I've modified the scenario in various other ways, and the responses are quite interesting. For example, students who identified as Christian rarely chose to save the dog (indeed, many responded with astonishment at the reactions of their classmates who chose to save the dog over the human). When the stranger was replaced with someone closer to the student (e.g., a family member), most students opted to save the human. When broken down by gender, across all cases female students were more likely than male students to save the dog.

2. Richard Topolski, J. Nicole Weaver, Zachary Martin, and Jason McCoy, "Choosing between the Emotional Dog and the Rational Pal: A Moral Dilemma with a Tail," *Anthrozoös* 26, no. 2 (2013): 253–263.

3. See Lyman Stone, "Fewer Babies, More Pets? Parenthood, Marriage, and Pet Ownership in America," *Institute for Family Studies*, November 15, 2017, https://ifstudies.org/blog/fewer-babies-more-pets-parenthood-marriage-and-pet-ownership-in-america. For a stern critique of this tendency, see G. Shane Morris, "Having Pets Instead of Kids Should Be Considered a Psychiatric Disorder," *The Federalist*, May 9, 2017, http://thefederalist.com/2017/05/09/pets-instead-kids-considered-psychiatric-disorder/.

4. This is well documented in Nancy Pearcey, *Saving Leonardo: A Call to Resist the Secular Assault on Mind, Morals, and Meaning* (Nashville: B&H Academic, 2010).

5. Peter Carruthers, "Animal Mentality: Its Character, Extent, and Moral Significance," in *The Oxford Handbook of Animal Ethics*, eds. R. Frey and T. Beauchamp (Oxford: Oxford University Press, 2011), 400.

6. Carruthers, "Animal Mentality," 401.

7. Topolski et al., "Choosing between the Emotional Dog and the Rational Pal," 258. The study found that women, who tend to form a stronger emotional bond with pets than do men and are "more likely to operate on a care-based moral reasoning system," were more likely than men to choose to

save their pet (M. Angantyr, J. Eklund, and E. M. Hansen, "A Comparison of Empathy for Humans and Empathy for Animals," *Anthrozoös* 24 [2011]: 369–377).

8. For many Christians, the answer is typically just "the Bible says so." This isn't a bad answer per se, but it will be of little help in trying to convince someone who doesn't already regard the Bible as authoritative.

9. This is documented in Wesley J. Smith, *The War on Humans* (Seattle: Discovery Institute Press, 2014), and *A Rat Is a Pig Is a Dog Is a Boy: The Human Costs of the Animal Rights Movement* (New York: Encounter, 2012). Within my own field of expertise (moral philosophy and applied ethics), a large majority of professors believe that animals have serious moral status and that meat-consumption, animal testing, and other practices in which we use animals to serve our needs are seriously immoral. One survey found that 60 percent of ethics professors rate meat-eating as morally bad. (Ironically, many of these same professors also reported that they privately eat meat in direct contradiction to what they say they believe.) See Eric Schwitzgebel and Joshua Rust, "The Moral Behavior of Ethics Professors: Relationships Among Self-Reported Behavior, Expressed Normative Attitude, and Directly Observed Behavior," *Philosophical Psychology* 27, no. 3 (2014): 293–327.

10. Jeff McMahan, "The Moral Problem of Predation," in *Philosophy Comes to Dinner: Arguments About the Ethics of Eating*, eds. A. Chignell, T. Cuneo, and M. Halteman (New York: Routledge, 2015), 268–294.

11. Jeff McMahan, *The Ethics of Killing: Problems at the Margins of Life* (Oxford: Oxford University Press, 2002).

12. Peter Singer, "Twenty Questions," *Journal of Practical Ethics* 4, no. 2 (2016): 67–78.

13. It is very important to note that I am talking about *Darwinian* evolution, not evolutionary theory in general. There are versions of evolution theory, such as theistic evolution and evolutionary creationism, that explicitly preserve the special difference between human beings and animals. That said, theistic evolution does face a number of challenges. See J. P. Moreland et al., eds., *Theistic Evolution: A Scientific, Philosophical, and Theological Critique* (Wheaton: Crossway, 2017).

14. James Rachels, *Created From Animals: The Moral Implications of Darwinism* (Oxford: Oxford University Press, 1990).

15. David Hull, *The Metaphysics of Evolution* (Albany: SUNY Press, 1989), 74–75.

16. E. O. Wilson, *Sociobiology: The New Synthesis* (Cambridge: Harvard University Press, 1980), 182.

17. Richard Dawkins, *The Selfish Gene*, 2nd ed. (New York: Houghton Mifflin, 2006), 200–201.

18. Daniel Dennett, *Breaking the Spell: Religion as a Natural Phenomenon* (New York: Viking, 2006), 4.

19. Richard Dawkins notes, "In a universe of … blind physical forces and genetic replication, some people are going to get hurt, other people are going to

get lucky, and you won't find any rhyme or reason in it, nor any justice. The universe we observe has precisely the properties we should expect if there is, at bottom, no design, no purpose, no evil and no good, nothing but blind, pitiless indifference … DNA neither knows nor cares. DNA just is. And we dance to its music" (*River Out of Eden: A Darwinian View of Life* [New York: Basic Books, 1995], 131–132).

20. See J. P. Moreland et al., eds., *Theistic Evolution*; Stephen C. Meyer, *Darwin's Doubt: The Explosive Origin of Animal Life and the Case for Intelligent Design* (Seattle: HarperOne, 2013); Douglas Axe, *Undeniable: How Biology Confirms Our Intuition That Life Is Designed* (Seattle: HarperOne, 2016); and Michael J. Behe, *Darwin Devolves: The New Science About DNA That Challenges Evolution* (Seattle: HarperOne, 2019).

21. For other approaches, see David Oderberg, *Real Essentialism* (New York: Routledge, 2008); and W. Norris Clarke, *The One and the Many: A Contemporary Thomistic Metaphysics* (Notre Dame: University of Notre Dame Press, 2011), chapter 15.

22. See Edward Feser, *Scholastic Metaphysics: A Contemporary Introduction* (Heusenstamm: Editiones Scholasticae, 2014), 6–30; and J. P. Moreland, *Scientism and Secularism: Learning to Respond to a Dangerous Ideology* (Wheaton: Crossway, 2018).

23. See George Bealer and Robert Koons, eds., *The Waning of Materialism* (Oxford: Oxford University Press, 2010); William Lane Craig and J. P. Moreland, eds., *Naturalism: A Critical Analysis* (New York: Routledge, 2000); Angus Menuge, *Agents Under Fire: Materialism and the Rationality of Science* (Lanham: Rowman and Littlefield, 2004); and Bruce Gordon and William Dembski, eds., *The Nature of Nature: Examining the Role of Naturalism in Science* (Wilmington: ISI Books, 2010).

24. Tom Regan, *The Case for Animal Rights* (Berkeley: University of California Press, 1983).

25. See David S. Oderberg, *Moral Theory: A Non-Consequentialist Approach* (Oxford: Blackwell, 2000).

26. See my other chapter in this book for a more detailed treatment.

27. The Green Revolution, which saved millions of lives around the world, is a great example of a responsible and wise use of the environment. Fossil fuels have also allowed for great strides in human development. See Alex Epstein, *The Moral Case for Fossil Fuels* (New York: Portfolio/Penguin, 2014); and Stephen Moore and Kathleen Hartnett White, *Fueling Freedom: Exposing the Mad War on Energy* (Washington: Regnery, 2016).

7. THE OLD TESTAMENT'S CASE FOR HUMANITY SUBDUING AND RULING OVER EVERY LIVING CREATURE BY WALTER C. KAISER JR.

1. This would be different from the more sophisticated version of utilitarianism as espoused by Princeton philosopher Peter Singer.

2. Especially noteworthy are the writings of Andrew A. Linzey: *Animal Rights: A Christian Assessment of Man's Treatment of Animals* (London: SCM Press Ltd., 1976), and *Animal Theology* (Chicago: University of Illinois Press, 1995).

3. Richard A. Young, *Is God a Vegetarian? Christianity, Vegetarian, and Animal Rights* (Chicago: Open Court, 1999), 127.

4. Lynn White Jr., "The Historical Roots of Our Ecologic Crisis," *Science* 155 (1967): 1203–1207.

8. VEGGIE TALES? PETA, PAGANISM, AND OTHER VEGAN CONFUSIONS BY PAUL COPAN

1. Bill Broadway, "A Meatless Mission: Group Says Jesus Didn't Eat Animals, Christians Should Follow Suit," *Washington Post*, March 13, 1999, https://www.washingtonpost.com/archive/local/1999/03/13/a-meatless-mission-group-says-jesus-didnt-eat-animals-christians-should-follow-suit/afca17ce-8657-4674-b243-e5922ce50630/?utm_term=.47822c79d049.

2. Charles Camosy, *For Love of Animals: Christian Ethics, Consistent Action* (Cincinnati: Franciscan Media, 2013), 129.

3. Camosy, *For Love of Animals*, 56. For a short synopsis, see Charles Camosy's article, "Why All Christians Should Go Vegan," *Washington Post*, January 5, 2017, https://www.washingtonpost.com/posteverything/wp/2017/01/05/why-all-christians-should-go-vegan/?utm_term=.d42068bc0f83.

4. Daniel Dombrowski, *The Philosophy of Vegetarianism* (Amherst: University of Massachusetts Press, 1984), 17.

5. Dombrowski, *The Philosophy of Vegetarianism*, 5.

6. Dombrowski, *The Philosophy of Vegetarianism*, 5.

7. For example, Robert Wennberg, *God, Humans, and Animals: An Invitation to Enlarge Our Moral Universe* (Grand Rapids: Eerdmans, 2002). Note that despite the late Wennberg's compassion towards animals, he did make allowance for the abortion of humans. See his *Life in the Balance* (Grand Rapids: Eerdmans, 1985).

8. Hannah Hurnard, *Eagles' Wings to the Higher Places* (New York: Harper and Row, 1983), 89, 90–91. Thanks to my wife, Jacqueline, for pointing out this reference.

9. On the flaws of "animal rights" and the *non-moral* status of animals, see David S. Oderberg, "The Illusion of Animal Rights," *Human Life Review* 26 (Spring/Summer 2000): 37–45. A brief excerpt can be found here: https://www.questia.com/magazine/1P3-57663676/the-illusion-of-animal-rights. For a more detailed argument against animal rights, see David Oderberg, *Applied Ethics: A Non-Consequentialist Approach* (Oxford: Blackwell, 2000). On the question of animal suffering, see Michael J. Murray, "Animal Pain," in *Dictionary of Christianity and Science*, eds. Paul Copan et al. (Grand Rapids: Eerdmans, 2017). For a more detailed discussion, see Michael Murray, *Nature Red in Tooth and Claw: Theism and the Problem of Animal Suffering* (New York: Oxford University Press, 2008).

10. See Roger Scruton, *Animal Rights and Wrongs,* 3rd ed. (London: Metro, 2000).

11. The Christian ethicist David Clough takes a less radical vegan perspective in chapter 2 of his *On Animals: Volume II: Theological Ethics* (Edinburgh: T&T Clark, 2018). Thanks to David Clough for sending me a copy of this chapter.

12. For a discussion of the many health benefits of meat-eating over against a strictly vegan diet, see the balanced presentation by Precision Nutrition's founder John Bernardi, PhD, "The Meat Debate: Good for Us or Disease Waiting to Happen?," accessed April 16, 2019, https://www.precisionnutrition.com/meat-and-health. See also "Eating Meat: Good or Bad for You?," *Authoritydiet.com*, September 29, 2018, https://www.authoritydiet.com/eating-meat-good-bad-you-health-benefits-myths-why/.

13. James Reichmann, *Evolution, Animal 'Rights,' and the Environment* (Washington: Catholic University of America Press, 2000), 368, 372.

14. "Joyful, Compassionate Eating," Christian Vegetarian Association, January 2016, https://christianveg.org/images/compassionate-eating-20180125.pdf, 3. On page 4, the document states, "In Genesis 2:18–19, God made animals as Adam's helpers and companions. The Bible repeatedly describes God's concern for animals and forbids cruelty." Actually, the very passage says that *none* of the animals proved a suitable help or partner for Adam. So God made the woman for the man. Animals are *not* partners of humans, according to Genesis. And this document conveniently ignores "cruel" passages related to the sacrificial system and many other biblical texts discussed in chapters 7 to 9 of this book. The booklet is shot through with theologically erroneous claims and misleading, selective uses of Scripture texts.

15. In addition to arguing for such predatory activity, Davis A. Young and Ralph F. Stearley argue for an ancient earth as well: *The Bible, Rocks and Time: Geological Evidence for the Age of the Earth* (Downers Grove: IVP Academic, 2008); see also Carol Hill et al., *The Grand Canyon: Monument to an Ancient Earth* (Grand Rapids: Kregel, 2016).

16. John Goldingay, *Old Testament Theology: Israel's Story*, vol. 1 (Downers Grove: InterVarsity Press, 2003), 111.

17. Goldingay, *Old Testament Theology*, 112.

9. WHAT WOULD JESUS EAT? FROM KOSHER TO EVERYTHING
BY PAUL COPAN

1. Mortimer Adler, "A Philosopher's Religious Faith," in *Philosophers Who Believe: The Spiritual Journeys of Eleven Leading Thinkers*, ed. Kelly James Clark (Downers Grove: InterVarsity Press, 1993), 215.

2. For a discussion of faith and reason, see Paul Copan, *A Little Book for New Philosophers* (Downers Grove: IVP Academic, 2016). For other resources, see www.paulcopan.com. See also Paul Gould, *Cultural Apologetics: Renewing the Christian Voice, Conscience and Imagination in a Disenchanted World* (Grand Rapids: Zondervan, 2019).

3. Peter J. Williams, *Can We Trust the Gospels?* (Wheaton: Crossway, 2018).

4. Craig Keener, *Miracles: The Credibility of the New Testament Accounts*, 2 vols. (Grand Rapids: Baker Academic, 2011).

5. See *The Dictionary of Christianity and Science*, eds. Paul Copan et al. (Grand Rapids: Zondervan, 2017).

6. For example, see Christian philosopher and theologian William Lane Craig's website www.reasonablefaith.org, and Ted Cabal, Paul Copan, J. P. Moreland, and Chad Brand, *The Apologetics Study Bible*, 2nd ed. (Nashville: B&H Academic, 2017).

7. "The Dignity of Living Beings with Regard to Plants: Moral Consideration of Plants for Their Own Sake," Federal Ethics Committee on Non-Human Biotechnology (ECNH), April 2008, https://www.ekah.admin.ch/inhalte/ekah-dateien/dokumentation/publikationen/e-Broschure-Wurde-Pflanze-2008.pdf.

8. Joel B. Green, *The Gospel of Luke*, The New International Commentary on the New Testament (Grand Rapids: Eerdmans, 1997), 483.

9. R. T. France, *The Gospel of Matthew*, The New International Commentary on the New Testament (Grand Rapids: Eerdmans, 2007), 268.

10. In Leviticus, both Israelites/native-born and *Gentiles*—"aliens who sojourn among them" (17:8, 10, 12, 13, 15; 18:26)—are prohibited from *making sacrifices to idols* (17:7–9; cf. 17:7: "goat demons"), from *eating blood* (17:10–12), *eating meat with blood in it* (17:13–16), and *sexual immorality* (18).

11. Craig Keener, *Acts: An Exegetical Commentary: 15:1-23:35*, vol. 3 (Grand Rapids: Baker Academic, 2014), 3126–43.

12. Andrew Linzey, *Animal Gospel* (Louisville: Westminster John Knox Press, 1998), 12.

13. "Joyful, Compassionate Eating," Christian Vegetarian Association, January 2016, https://christianveg.org/images/compassionate-eating-20180125.pdf, 3.

14. "Joyful, Compassionate Eating," 3.

10. SCRIPTURE AND SWINE: DOES SCRIPTURE ALLOW ME TO RAISE PIGS FOR FOOD? BY GORDON SPRONK AND RANDY SPRONK

1. For an exposition and application of Psalm 23, see Dallas Willard, *A Life without Lack: Living in the Fullness of Psalm 23* (Nashville: Thomas Nelson, 2018).

2. Dallas Willard discusses "Life in the Spirit" on YouTube videos, August 2018, https://www.youtube.com/watch?v=uBbHa2a9bKs.

CASTLE QUAY BOOKS

ALL OF OUR BOOKS ARE AVAILABLE AT
WWW.CASTLEQUAYBOOKS.COM.